convertible houses

houses
Convertible

Amanda Lam
and
Amy Thomas

Gibbs Smith, Publisher
To ENRICH AND INSPIRE HUMANKIND

Salt Lake City | Charleston | Santa Fe | Santa Barbara

First Edition
11 10 09 08 07   5 4 3 2 1

Published by
Gibbs Smith, Publisher
PO Box 667
Layton, Utah 84041

Orders: 1.800.835.4993
www.gibbs-smith.com

Designed by Debra McQuiston
Printed and bound in Hong Kong

Library of Congress Cataloging-in-Publication Data

Lam, Amanda.
  Convertible houses / Amanda Lam, Amy Thomas. — 1st ed.
     p. cm.
  ISBN-13: 978-1-4236-0029-9
  ISBN-10: 1-4236-0029-0
  1. Room layout (Dwellings) 2. Interior decoration. 3. Interior
architecture. I. Thomas, Amy. II. Title.

NK2113.L355 2007
747—dc22

2006024563

From the moment we met Suzanne and Alison in New York, to when Amanda and I submitted the manuscript, it was a thrilling project. Thanks to all three of you, and every talented architect and designer in between.

Thanks also to Mom, Dad, Amee, Chris, Dana, Julie, and everyone else who shared my excitement along the way. Thanks most of all to Fou for sparking my writing passion ten years ago, and for always being there.

—Amy

My heartfelt gratitude to the angels who helped me see this project through. Mom, Dad, Michelle, Christine, Jon, Lowen, Hector, without your love and support, this book would still be a jumble of notes and ideas in my head.

Amy, I couldn't have asked for a more amazing partner in crime. You kept me going through every valley.

To the architects, designers, photographers, and staff who took the time to share their vision and talent for this book, you are the true stars who gave this project life.

Gibbs Smith and Suzanne Taylor, thank you for taking a chance on two new authors and steering us to the pinpoint focus for this work.

—Amanda

01

contents

foreword

Convertible: *adj.*: **designed to be changed from one use or form to another.**

When you make New York City your home, there are certain comforts you relinquish and many decisions you make along the way. Is a sofa or dining table more important? Should that corner be home to a computer station or my ever-expanding shoe collection? How can I entertain five friends in my living room without having them realize that we're also sitting in my bedroom/home office?

These are the types of questions both of us have grappled with. But rather than learning to do without, we've gotten creative with our limited spaces. And in the midst of wrestling where to fit our desks and how to comfortably accommodate visiting friends, the ideas for this book were being stored in our heads.

While *Convertible Houses* was inspired by our personal trials and tribulations with city living, we know that tiny apartments aren't the only place where flexibility is key. Squeezing as much use as possible from your space is an important consideration, no matter how much square footage you have. For example, as more people embrace loft-style living, they realize there are many hurdles that come with leaving behind traditional room dividers. Practical considerations like privacy, storage, and space hierarchy inevitably rear their head.

And it's not just physical constraints that have changed the way we lay out our homes. The way we live has evolved, too. Gone are the days when walls literally defined functions within a household. Wireless computers are now dragged from the kitchen counter to the living room couch to a formal working area. Children can be supervised in the living room while dinner is being prepared in the kitchen. As the roles that we've assigned to rooms in the past become less rigid, it's all about getting the most bang out of your blueprint.

Multitasking is a buzzword we're all personally and professionally familiar with—why shouldn't we ask our homes to be just as hardworking? When you have a finite amount of space to work with, the only choice is to make it do double duty. Whether that means using a dining table that functions as a home office outside of mealtimes, or creating a sleeping platform overhead to make space for a couch below, there are creative ways to expand your living space without physically expanding your home.

The houses and apartments in this book will show you how to enjoy more functionality in a finite amount of space, as well as how to use specific devices to differentiate the activities that take place there. Good space planning means not only having a home for every object, but a place for every task—a challenge no matter where we live.

As with anything, it helps to start by being inspired. In Section 01, we've pulled together eleven homes from around the world that show inventive and stunning examples of convertible living. Some are quite tiny, as in the 655-square-foot Manhattan studio designed by AvroKO. And some are grand, like Jacques Van Haren's 4,844-square-foot Duplex Neuilly apartment.

In Section 02, we zoom in on some of the most successful strategies used in these homes. From installing curtain walls to divide a room for different uses, to adding a mezzanine in an apartment with high ceilings to create more living space, we share a range of tried-and-true devices that maximize space.

Lastly, we've included a good dose of practical information and professional tips that anyone can use. We believe you can enjoy convertible living no matter where you are or what your budget is. These simple ideas from renowned architects and design experts will show you the way.

We hope that whatever kind of space you live in, you'll find ideas in these pages that you can use to make your own home more functional and more comfortable. Sometimes trading up doesn't mean adding on—it just means finding ways to make everything work harder.

—Amanda and Amy

Pull out floor-to-ceiling drawers and everything, from a full-functioning kitchen to a hidden bedroom to stairs that take you to other levels in the house, is revealed.

The personality of each room can be radically altered with the simple act of opening or closing a sliding panel.

A movable wall was built on a custom pulley-and-track system that creates an instant guest room in the space between the kitchen and the bathroom.

Eleven inventive examples of convertible living

Shanghai chic in midtown Manhattan

CURTAIN APARTMENT

The Apartment
New York, NY
3,500 square feet

Most homeowners agree: renovations are never quick, easy, or painless. "If I had known what I was getting into, I never would have done it," laughs Cindy Gallop, a New York art collector. But when a historic YMCA building was converted into residential units in 2005, the allure of 3,500 square feet in the middle of Manhattan was too good to pass up; she bought the condo that would need a complete rehaul.

"I adore open-space living," Gallop declares. But as practical as she is creative, Gallop also acknowledges there are issues to loft-living. "It's very important to have the feel of open space, but also to have privacy when I need it." After all, she says, "God is not the only one watching." The ebullient homeowner knew weekend guests might appreciate the simple privacy that doors afford. It just so happened that

Stefan Boublil and Gina Alvarez, founders of the design firm The Apartment, were also charter owners in the converted YMCA building. It wasn't long before Gallop tapped the designing duo to add a good dose of practicality to her new home.

Once the condo, which had been the men's locker room in its former YMCA life, was demolished, The Apartment had a clean slate to play with. Gallop wanted the space to flow. And with an eclectic collection of art, Asian antiques, taxidermy, and fashion collectibles, she also wanted to maximize the square footage. In addition to these parameters, Gallop challenged the team to make her home look like a Shanghai nightclub. "What if it felt like the inside of a black piano?" marveled

Boublil, and thus a chic, black monochrome concept was born.

Because of Gallop's affinity for openness ("if you're lucky enough to have a lot of space in New York City, you want to do the classic loft-living," she points out), the team opted not to construct walls. But to fulfill the need for privacy, they installed curtain walls— 89 feet of them. This creates two curtainable areas in the home: one that closes off the master bathroom and bedroom, and another that separates the home theater into a private room that can be turned over to guests. Whether the curtains remain open or are drawn closed, the apartment maintains a seamless look because the walls, ceilings, and curtain tracking are all black. To make the curtains work twice as hard, Boublil and Alvarez used both a sheer panel ("it looks nice with candles behind it," says Gallop) »19

01

01 Even from the bedroom, which is located at the far corner, Gallop can view her entire condo when the curtain walls are left open.

02 The main room extends into the home theater/guest bedroom when the curtains remain open.

03 With the curtains partially drawn, the home has a sense of comfort: both privacy and open space prevail.

04

04 Looking into the bathroom from the other side, the sheer curtain is a soft barrier.

05, 06, 07 With the sheer curtain drawn, the loft is still open to views from the decadent bathtub. When the heavier curtain is drawn, there's instant privacy.

05

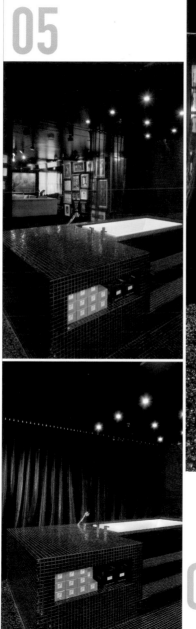

06

07

08 Gallop gets to show off her impressive shoe collection on a two-tier, backlit shelf that runs the length of the 72-foot-long main room. It's a whimsical storage solution that's right at home with Gallop's artsy sensibilities.

09 The Apartment built custom closets around two cement support pillars that couldn't be moved. Gallop makes good use of the eight new walls this provided (look at all that art!), as well as the interior space, which is used for storing paintings.

10 The Apartment marked the edge of the curtains with red so Gallop and her guests can easily find where to pass through.

and a heavier, sound-protective velvet panel ("it closes the room both visually and aurally," Boublil explains).

Besides privacy, the other challenge of open-space living is storage—which, as an avid art and shoe collector, is essential to Gallop. "I've got a big art collection, and that requires wall space," she says. The condo has two cement support pillars that couldn't be moved, so The Apartment simply built storage closets around them. This not only provided eight new walls on which Gallop can hang her art, but a safe, dry space for the paintings to be stored. As for Gallop's shoe collection, a more imaginative solution was divined: running the full length of the 72-foot-long main room, they built a two-tier, backlit shelf. On it, Gallop displays her hundreds of pairs of shoes.

Because of the artistic bent that already exists within the home, this practical solution is an ingenious aesthetic choice.

As a first-time experiment with curtaining walls, the designers were pleased with the results. "I was very positively surprised by how much the room changes when you open up the curtains," says Boubil, who founded The Apartment with Alvarez in 2001. "It takes on a new feeling."

More importantly, as the owner-occupant, Gallop is also happy with her flexible arrangements. After the nearly two years it took to design and transform the condo, Gallop is right at home in her Shanghai space—where, more often than not, the curtains are open. After all, she says, "I do like being able to look around and see my life around me."

CURTAIN APARTMENT SHOWS US:

» Privacy in bathroom and master bedroom.
» Transformation of home theater to guest bedroom.
» Reduction of sound throughout home.

DESIGN FIRM: The Apartment
FOUNDED: 2001
MEMBERS: 10
ADDRESS: 101 Crosby Street, New York, NY 10012
PHONE: 212.219.3661
WEBSITE: www.theapt.com
DRIVING PHILOSOPHY: Telling a compelling story with a beginning, middle, and end is the cornerstone of any design project, even if it's told in a different order.
PHOTOGRAPHY: Michael Weber

More than meets the eye

Draughtzman
Hong Kong, China
900 square feet

When none of the rooms in a home are large enough to contain its individual function, what is the most logical solution? Remove all the walls so that each task can borrow square footage from the others. Then, like a chameleon, the apartment can transform itself to best suit the task at hand, be it entertaining a large group or working solo on a painting.

This was the case for Evelyna Yee-Woo Liang, an artist who teaches at Hong Kong Polytechnic. She wanted the space to function as a quiet place to work on her art, as well as accommodate the occasional cocktail party when she staged a show there.

The 900-square-foot apartment was originally three small rooms connected by one long hallway. The chopped-up space felt cramped and ill suited »23

01

01 Stationary walls are replaced by folding panels to allow the square footage in this apartment to multitask.

02 The panels enclosing the kitchen are not only aesthetically pleasing but practical as well. The frosted glass is low maintenance and easy to clean.

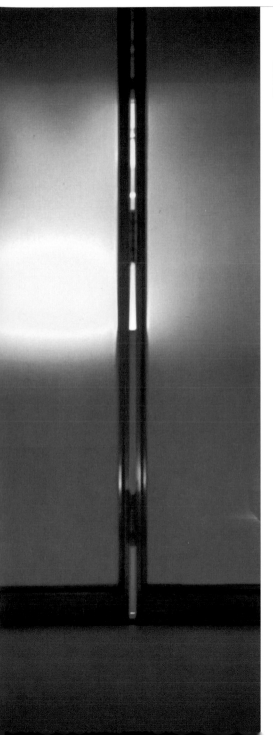

02

for anything more elaborate than accommodating a twin bed or a small breakfast table.

Craving a more open feeling in the space and room to stretch out, Yee-Woo Liang turned to two of her former students. Since leaving Hong Kong Polytechnic, Alliot Cheng and Ziggy Koo had opened Draughtzman, their own design studio, gaining attention with an Asia Pacific Interior Design Award and several accolades at the Hong Kong Designers Association show. They not only linked their future in business, they were also married shortly after graduating. With their mated vision, Yee-Woo Liang knew the duo would deliver the kind of creative space she was seeking.

Eager to craft a unique solution for their former mentor, Cheng and Koo began by eliminating every interior wall in the apartment to reduce the space to a clean rectangular box. Says Alliot, "We decided the intervening wall should be removed to release the penetration of daylight and reinstate the panoramic view overlooking the city."

Drawing their inspiration from the views of the intersecting rooftops in the city below, Draughtzman proceeded to put the apartment back together like a jigsaw puzzle, creating pieces that could neatly fit together and maximize the available space.

The main organizing feature Draughtzman inserted back into the room is an activity wall that divides the apartment into two halves. On one side, a set of hinged, orange glass doors fold back to reveal a kitchen running the length of the wall. When Yee-Woo Liang is cooking, the living room becomes part of the workspace, but once »25

03

04

the dishes are put away, the frosted-glass doors slide back and the space becomes a tranquil living room again, with all signs of cooking neatly stowed away. To make the closed device an asset rather than an awkward side-bar to the room, the entire box lights up from within, creating a vibrant focal point and an additional source of lighting in the room.

On the other side of the divider is a wall of shelving contained behind large glass doors. This bookends the main living space in the apartment, where some of the more inventive ideas in the apartment were implemented. The most dramatic is a set of cement-faced, swing-fold partitions. Using an inexpensive and rustic material that would create a neutral backdrop for Yee-Woo Liang's artwork, Draughtzman created a partition that swings away from the wall to form a partial divider in the space. Or when a pocket door

03 Frosted orange glass panels conceal the kitchen. Yee-Woo Liang loves strong colors, and Draughtzman used shades like orange and chartreuse to punctuate the more neutral spaces where Yee-Woo Liang's artwork could be displayed.

04 By illuminating the kitchen while the panels are closed, the glowing orange box turns into a focal point in the room.

05

is extended from the partition, it creates a third room that is completely private.

Along the wall where the partitions fold out, Draughtzman located the two bathrooms and additional storage. Two sliding cement doors provide an aesthetically pleasing and efficient way to access the bathrooms, while reducing the number of doorways that interrupt the flow of the wall.

The flat is blessed with four large bay windows. To emphasize the view, Draughtzman expanded the sills in front of each, creating a perch for sitting or resting a plate during a party, as well as extra space for storage underneath. "It would be a waste if we left them just as they were," says Cheng. "They could be extended to serve as contemplation chambers."

In front of the largest window in the apartment, Draughtzman created a platform large enough to accommodate a Japanese-style tearoom setup for dining. To add even more functionality, the platform is the same width as a double bed. When guests come over, Yee-Woo Liang can pull out the futons stored underneath and turn the area into a guest room.

To outfit the apartment, the furniture needed to be just as transformable as the space itself. Draughtzman designed a series of furniture they named "cookies." A daybed, chair, desk, lounger, and stool are all incorporated into the system, which can fold together as a compact, freestanding island in the center of the space when ≫29

05 An extra-wide sill forms a place that feels removed from the rest of the apartment for contemplating the view. With the addition of a futon, it becomes a sleeping platform for guests.

06 A cement-faced partition can swing into the room dividing it in half to create smaller spaces for lounging and working. At the far end, glass doors keep shelves dust free while also drawing the eye up to the ceiling.

06

07

08

07 The bathroom is accessed through a sliding door with the same cement facing as the swinging partition. Using a sliding door versus a traditional door eliminates the need for clearance to open into the room.

08 Different hues of glass distinguish the windows and add an artful element. Here, the "cookies" are in their most compact arrangement, fitting together into a rectangle that provides space for lounging and resting drinks at a party.

Yee-Woo Liang has clients over to the apartment for an art show, or pull apart into individual pieces that can be scattered throughout the apartment to suit her needs. "'Cookies' create a landscape for sitting, writing, reading, resting, sleeping, and for social seating," says Cheng. Built on aluminum frames, the pieces are light. Each piece has caster wheels, so it easily rolls to any area in the apartment. When Yee-Woo Liang's friends come over, they often "rearrange 'cookies' in their own way," remarks Alliot. In this sense, "'cookies' are an art installation in the space, with people gathered around, leaning and lying, talking and laughing. We think 'cookies' have performed their duty." It's all a fitting setting for the artist who happily makes her creative nest here.

ARTIST'S APARTMENT SHOWS US:

» Swinging partitions provide a flexible way to divide space.
» Castors allow furniture to be easily moved anywhere in the apartment.
» Locating a kitchen behind folding doors prevents it from intruding on the rest of the space outside of mealtimes.

DESIGN FIRM: Draughtzman
FOUNDED: 2000
MEMBERS: 2
ADDRESS: G/F, 39 North York, Siu Lek Yuen, Shatin, N.T., Hong Kong
PHONE: 852.2866.2112
FAX: 852.2861.2831
DRIVING PHILOSOPHY:
Going across disciplines: Active integration of multiple disciplines can release the hidden potential constrained in the separation of disciplines.
Reunifying stratification: Good design solutions are the result of the thoughtful consideration of the whole design process from conceptual development to construction administration.
Beyond decorative skin: We don't go for a particular style, as the specific nature of the project and client will provide the unique base of the design.

A gathering place in Paris

Jacques Van Haren
Paris, France
4,844 square feet

A polished masterpiece duplex in the heart of Paris is bound to be the site of many different kinds of gatherings. From intimate pairings to colorful parties for forty, this apartment slips neatly into a wide array of settings.

The couple living here purchased the apartment while the building was undergoing a gut renovation. They brought in architect Jacques Van Haren to create a family home that would take advantage of the large quarters they had acquired in Neuilly, one of the best neighborhoods in Paris.

Having suffered through a previous apartment that was dark and parceled off, the couple asked Van Haren to create as much visual space as possible in their new home. As it was still an early stage in the building's reworking, Van Haren was able to greatly

01

influence the layout. "The team, which was working on the building, allowed us to intervene during the conception phase. This allowed us to modify load-bearing walls, divert utilitarian spaces, and delocalize the kitchen and bathrooms. Even the stairs could be placed exactly where we would have wished to position it," says the architect.

Van Haren wanted to open up the ground floor as much as possible. "We had to work on the space in order to have only a few visual obstacles if we turn our heads 360 degrees," notes Van Haren. The idea was to achieve a fluid movement through the space and create sight lines that would allow the eye to travel well beyond the immediate room. A tight color palette of slick whites and light woods further emphasizes the feeling. The first floor is awash with light, natural stone, while blond oak floors

run throughout the bedrooms. White walls and white-lacquered built-ins reflect light from every surface throughout the home.

When the family saw that the design had the potential to change the way they lived, they quickly went from expecting a beautiful design to pushing for new kinds of functionality. "Very quickly, they started to be excited even on the basis of very simple ideas drawn in rough sketches. This enthusiasm encouraged us to go even further in our ideas," says Van Haren.

The large living space, which Van Haren refers to as the "heart of life" for the home, is open to the adjacent dining space, allowing for easy flow from cocktails to dinner. So as not to intrude on the living room, but still create a place for the stone staircase to be showcased, the front hallway to the »35

01 Van Haren eliminated all unnecessary dividers and barriers on the ground floor to create as much light and open space as possible. Even the doors between the living room and the stairwell are made of transparent glass to enhance visibility.

02 Strong lines and the use of large expanses of singular materials lend a dramatic quality to Van Haren's spaces. Here in the dining room, a rich wenge wood covers a focal wall. Wenge wood also provides the material for the dining table, chairs, and an accent mirror.

02

04

03

03 Three pivoting glass doors allow this space to be completely open for circulation, or to form a transparent wall between the living room and the upstairs while still allowing light and sight lines to flow through.

04 White walls, white floors, and white-lacquered cabinetry bounce light off every surface. The uniform color also helps to lead the eye from one space to the next.

05 Once the sliding panel to the kitchen is shut, the casual breakfast nook takes on an intimate scale and connection to the outdoors that differs vastly from the polished opulence of the rest of the apartment.

05

stairs was made extra large and brightly lit.

As entertaining is an important activity for the family, having a way to distinguish the public from private spaces in the home was important. A series of three pivoting glass doors in front of the stairs effectively forms a transparent wall to the upstairs when shut. Light and sight lines are allowed to flow freely, but the doors provide a way to close off access to more personal areas in the house. When

meals are being prepared, it's also helpful for keeping kitchen smells contained.

Controlling movement and passageways within the home was a key element of Van Haren's design. Large, sliding pocket doors are used to discreetly hide doorways throughout the apartment. Van Haren uses them to close off the traffic between spaces as if there were no connections between the rooms to begin with. Between the kitchen and dining room, a sliding panel, covered in the same rich wenge wood as the focal wall of the dining room, closes seamlessly, so that all traces of the kitchen are hidden from view. Between the casual dining space and the other end of the kitchen, another large white pocket door closes off that space, creating a serene white box for dining. The personality of each room can be radically altered with the

06

simple act of opening or closing a sliding panel.

The largest partition in the house is actually in the master bedroom. Reaching from floor to ceiling and spanning the width of one-third of the room, the sliding panels transform the room into a huge en suite when open, connecting the lavish master bathroom with the sleeping area. The use of sliding doors allows the owners to instantly double the size of the space, or create a more intimate enclosure by keeping the rooms independent.

To accommodate a roster of overnight guests in this well-frequented city, the couple asked for many of the rooms to have the double function of converting to a guest room. The children's playroom contains a bed with a tight slipcover that functions as a

sofa by day and a bed for visitors at night. A large drawer that runs the length of the bed provides storage for extra bedding and blankets while maximizing the space below. To decrease clutter in the minimalist room, a built-in desk functions both as bureau and makeshift workspace.

Down the hall, a study also houses a convertible sofa bed. It's the ideal place for a catnap during long work sessions, or for extra overnight guests. Behind a wall of storage, Van Haren was able to find space for a guest shower. When visitors are not around, a discreet pocket door makes the bathing area appear like an extension of the closet.

Wherever possible, Van Haren built the room's functional needs into the »38

06 Sliding panels—covered in the same warm oak as the floor and bed—run floor to ceiling between the bedroom and the bathroom. The volume of the room instantly doubles when the doors are open between the two.

07 To accommodate frequent guests, the owners needed as many extra sleeping areas as possible. Here in the children's playroom, a slim bed also functions as a lounge seat. An extra-wide drawer below stows extra bedding and toys.

07

08

architecture. In the study, the storage, desks, and even sofa bed are part of the interior architecture, while the den has a wall of storage facing custom sofas that maximize seating in the room. This tight synchronization of the architecture and the furnishings ensures the most efficient use of the space, while also keeping the design consistent from every aspect. Van Haren notes, "Under these conditions, it was rather interesting to be in charge of the coordination of all the different working teams. In 1998, this style [of collaboration] was rather rare." For an architect with a very specific vision, being able to attend to every detail—down to the side chairs and wardrobes—allows him to drive his design into every interaction between the homeowners and the space.

"At the beginning, the couple who had contacted us had not considered [that the design would] transform so substantially the way they live," says Van Haren. The flexible guest accommodations have made it easy for them to play host to out-of-towners, while the open layout with its focus on the living area has created a central place for them to gather as a family or with friends. "They underestimated the impact of our project and the changes it would bring compared to more traditional apartments." The result? The finished apartment is a finely honed design that has not only radically changed the space, but also the behavior of the family living within.

08 To reduce visual clutter, Van Haren located all of the media and storage in the den behind a wall of sleek white doors. To maximize the footprint of the room, he designed custom sofas that perfectly fill the space.

DUPLEX NEUILLY SHOWS US:

» Uniform colors and surfaces help spaces flow into each other and lengthen sight lines.
» Sliding doors allow transitions between rooms to be seamlessly closed off.
» All extra rooms in a home can be made into convertible guest rooms.

DESIGN FIRM: Jacques Van Haren with Axel Verhoustraeten
FOUNDED: 1998
MEMBERS: 5
ADDRESS: 9 Avenue du Vert Chasseur, Brussels 1180, Belgium
PHONE: 32.2.511.54.43
WEBSITE: www.jacquesvanharen.com
DRIVING PHILOSOPHY: A new approach to luxury with the use of exceptional materials and fully integrated design. Our main aspiration is to limit the decorating element within the creation and offer to our clients a program focusing on volumes, which are almost self-sufficient and already include most of the vital functions.
PHOTOGRAPHY: Gregoire Semal

Open to possibility

Nendo
Tokyo, Japan
1,744 square feet

Perhaps nowhere else in the world is space a greater commodity than in Tokyo. While almost everyone in Japan lives in homes that are less than 1,000 square feet, housing is even more limited in the capital city—a fact not lost on Oki Sato, founder of the Japanese architectural firm nendo.

While living in the city with his parents and siblings, Sato realized that he and his family used the common living room for everything and reserved their bedrooms for sleep. So when Sato set to work on designing a new home for his family, he wanted to maximize the main living area. And with the Drawer House, he maximized space in a most simple but clever way.

"The residential functions [of the Drawer House] are condensed into one side of the wall," explains »43

01

02

03

nendo's Takahiro Matsumura, "and can be pulled out when necessary, like drawers." This keeps the space clean and streamlines the home's functionality. On the ground level, for example, an open living area with slate floors looks elegant with white ash doors that run the length of the room. But pull out the floor-to-ceiling drawers and everything, from a full-functioning kitchen to a hidden bedroom to stairs that take you to other levels in the house, is revealed. "It's a simple mechanism, but this adaptive and flexible space is very effective in the limited housing situation in Tokyo," Matsumura points out.

01 Stairs going up to the second level, the kitchen, and actual drawers for storing items are some of the surprises revealed behind the ash wall.

02 The entire left wall of the Drawer House is lined with drawers and doors that conceal rooms and furniture.

03 Natural light bathes the entrance of the Drawer House.

04

05

Sato carried the concept throughout the home. From the outside, the Drawer House looks rather innocuous with a facade that could hide a small factory or workspace. But the plain exterior on a small Tokyo cul-de-sac belies living quarters that encompass three stories, 1,744 square feet, and 18 habitable drawers. On the second floor, the extended drawers reveal more intimate structures such as beds, bookshelves, and even a bathtub. The main living room has a softer look, thanks to oak floors and the same white ash drawers that reveal two bunk beds, as well as a work area with a desk, chair, and shelves. »49

04 The Sato family has plenty of open living space when the drawers are "put away" and the main floor is unoccupied.

05 Drawers and casters make moving items around a breeze.

06 A retractable glass wall extends the main room on the second floor outdoors, providing much needed space.

06

07, 08, 09 The pullout features on the second floor of the Drawer House reveal more personal items, such as beds, a desk, and shelves.

10, 11 Bunk beds that are tucked away behind the wall also extend, thanks to the use of casters.

12 Even guests get their own sleeping alcove with all the functionality packed into the Drawer House.

11

10

12

The room is further transformed and even more space is optimized when a wall-to-wall glass door is opened, extending the living space onto an outdoor terrace.

Sato started nendo, which means "clay" in Japanese, in 2002, with the idea of bringing free design and flexible thinking to his space-crunched clients. "Our motto is to be free-formed, flexible, and adaptable in the design scene." Every one of these characteristics is readily apparent in the Drawer House.

While adaptable architecture is a practical design approach in a city like Tokyo, there's also a strong emotional component to nendo's projects. "Every design needs the balance between fascination and flavor. Both the fun and beauty, which appeal to the emotional right part of the brain, and the cost, function, and concept, which appeal to the logical left part of the brain, are very important elements of our work."

In the case of the Drawer House, you can't help but fall in love with the whimsical solution for crowded living. The drawers enable the space to be flexible, accommodating functions like cooking and sleeping, as well as benign storage and display devices.

"The messages behind our designs are important in our wide field of design. Though it is different how one may feel, we would like to emphasize creating conversations between objects and people."

"Our goal is not to create best sellers or masterpieces, but to start a new trend," the architect states. "We wish to launch designs that have potential for generating enormous force, like a snowflake causing an avalanche." Which, in the case of the Drawer House, could be an open-and-shut case.

DRAWER HOUSE SHOWS US:

» Seamless transitions between living and functional space.
» Maximized use of limited floor space.
» Extra storage.

DESIGN FIRM: nendo
FOUNDED: 2002
MEMBERS: 10
ADDRESS: 4-1-20-2A Mejiro Toshima-ku, Tokyo 171-0031 Japan
PHONE: 81.(0)3.3954.5554
FAX: 81.(0)3.3954.5581
WEBSITE: www.nendo.jp
DRIVING PHILOSOPHY: To be flexible and adaptable to design with passionate ideas and breakthrough solutions.
PHOTOGRAPHY:
Nacasa & Partners

Where can a fellow catch some zzz's?

THE Z-BOX

Dan Hisel Design
Lynn, MA
1,450 square feet

Space, as a concept, can be applied to many realms: astronomy, psychology, and, of course, architecture and design. For most of us, space—as in living space—comes down to square footage. Dan Hisel, founder and principal of Dan Hisel Design in Cambridge, Massachusetts, takes it a step further. "I've always been interested in blurring the boundaries of architecture—what architecture can be when it comes to human interaction," reflects the architect. In 2004, he had an opportunity to intimately explore the concept of people's relationship with space when his former neighbors approached him with a job.

Robert and Janice Fathman were quite pleased with the loft they were closing on in Lynn, Massachusetts. And with 1,450 square feet, 13-foot

01

ceilings, clean, white walls, and great light, they had every reason to be. But even so, the couple realized their dream home had one key issue: they had nowhere to sleep (save for the vault, which, as a former insurance office, came with the loft). "We fell in love with the space, but there's no privacy," says Robert. As soon as they enlisted Hisel, the three of them started thinking about the best way to solve the issue.

One thing they immediately agreed on was that they didn't want to build a sleeping area out of Sheetrock—it just wouldn't feel right in the loft. "Initially, I wanted to do something with glass blocks," Robert remembers. "But we looked at the price of it, and it was more than we were

willing to spend." Although the couple's priority was to create a private place for sleeping, Hisel also recognized that Robert and Janice would need bookshelves, closets, lighting, and other practical necessities that are often absent in lofts. They needed something that would accommodate not just one function (sleeping), but meet several needs (storage, style, and seamlessness).

Since the loft was clean and white, "very much like a blank canvas," Hisel knew he could create something completely distinct to complement the raw space. "The idea of building a freestanding object was always a preliminary idea for me. I didn't see any point in trying to blend the new building with the existing loft," Hisel explains. In the end, his solution was something he

01 Closets line one wall, providing the newlywed couple with ample storage.

02 The entryway to the Z-Box, which includes both sheer and velvet curtains, marks a subtle transition into the living space.

02

dubbed Furnitecture. "It's a silly word that indicates the hybridization of those two typically distinct practices," he says. "In the Z-Box, I saw an opportunity to take architecture and kind of get it to do some of the work that furniture typically does." In this case, in his words, that is Bed + Shelves + Closets + Storage + Lamp + Dog Bed = Z-Box.

The Z-Box—named for the universal sign of snoring, or "catching some zzz's"—is a 12 x 12-foot freestanding cube. "[It] solves two problems facing the owners," the architect explains. "Where are we going to sleep and where are we going to put all this stuff?" The interior is crafted out of beautiful Douglas fir, which creates a warm, cozy environment for

03

the Fathmans to inhabit. And, exploring his concept of people's relationship with space, Hisel designed the form and functions of the Z-Box to be and feel intuitive. The custom-built headboard, for example, tilts back so when the couple sits up in bed to read, it's at a natural angle. Additionally, the walls are "carved up" with shelves on either side of the bed. When Robert or Janice reaches over to take or place something on a shelf, it's as if they're pushing into the wall. "The architecture is deflecting in response to human activity," Hisel explains.

By using an interior wood frame and an exterior steel frame, Hisel created a cavity in the box wide enough to place a dozen incandescent lights that are controlled with dimmers. When the lights are off, the Z-Box's exterior "skin," made with perforated steel and polycarbonate, is an artistic spectacle. "It's beautiful to look at," says Robert of the prismatic patterns that are revealed when natural light reflects off the metal. When the lights are flicked on, the box takes on a totally different aesthetic: the walls glow like a lantern, becoming semitransparent screens through which shadows and silhouettes are seen.

"People *can* have an intimate relationship with architecture," Hisel insists—which is exactly what the Fathmans have with the Z-Box. It's given the newlywed couple a cozy place to sleep and practical space to hold personal »58

03 The custom-built Douglas fir interior provides subtracted space for lights, shelves, a headboard, and bedside tables. It's small, but warm and cozy.

04

04 The perforated steel and polycarbonate "skin" of the Z-Box mesmerizes with prismatic patterns when the lights are off.

05 The walls become semi-transparent screens when the lights are on, revealing shadows and silhouettes from within the Z-Box.

05

06

07

belongings. Every little detail was given great thought. In addition to the shelves on the inside, the exterior walls are dotted with shelves, giving Robert and Janice a place to display books, pictures, art, and other personal items. But the Z-Box's coup de grace is the built-in dog bed for Hank and Lily, two very lucky pugs.

08

**THE Z-BOX
SHOWS US:**

» Private and cozy room for sleeping.
» Concealed storage in exposed loft.
» Separation of open living area and private art studio.

DESIGN FIRM: Dan Hisel Design
FOUNDED: 2002
MEMBERS: 4
ADDRESS: 238 Columbia Street, #2N, Cambridge, MA 02139
PHONE: 617.547.3151
WEBSITE:
www.danhiseldesign.com
DRIVING PHILOSOPHY: Founded on a commitment to architecture as a poetic art, Dan Hisel strives to create innovative contemporary designs that sensitively integrate our bodily experiences with the rich variety of environments that surround us.
PHOTOGRAPHY:
Peter Vanderwarker

06 The freestanding cube offers concealed storage, open display areas, and privacy for catching some zzz's.

07 Hank and Lily, the pugs, get their own resident space within the Z-Box's studio wall.

08 A close-up of an exterior wall shows how Janice and Robert can use the storage areas to display fun, personal objects. The storage areas are both practical and decorative.

Let the guests arrive

AvroKO
New York, NY
655 square feet

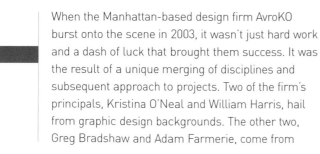

When the Manhattan-based design firm AvroKO burst onto the scene in 2003, it wasn't just hard work and a dash of luck that brought them success. It was the result of a unique merging of disciplines and subsequent approach to projects. Two of the firm's principals, Kristina O'Neal and William Harris, hail from graphic design backgrounds. The other two, Greg Bradshaw and Adam Farmerie, come from architecture. As the foursome, who met as college friends, found themselves collaborating on projects over the years, they realized their symbiotic relationship meant something: approaching design in a holistic way yields more inventive—and incredibly successful—results.

Part and parcel of AvroKO's unique background and philosophy is their devotion to a "self-propelled"

project each year—that is, they take on one project themselves, including funding, so there are no client restrictions. "It's a way for us to work and experiment as much as we need to," explains O'Neal. Public, the restaurant that put them on the map with the James Beard awards for Outstanding Restaurant Design and Outstanding Restaurant Graphics, had been their self-propelled project in 2004. In 2005, it was smart.space.

Smart.space was the transformation of an ordinary studio apartment in Greenwich Village into a home that combines high style, green living, and clever design. While undeniably chic and high-concept, smart.space was really borne out of practicality. "Space efficiency is definitely

the dominant theme," O'Neal says. AvroKO partnered with the apartment's owner, fully intending to resell it. Then, with the goal of giving New Yorkers more comfort in cramped quarters, the firm spent over nine months redesigning the compact space to make it more functional.

"We just talked to everyone we knew about their biggest challenges and needs," O'Neal explains of their initial planning phase. One prominent theme they discovered was the desire for extra space for overnight guests, a common occurrence in a popular city like New York. "Even with people who have an extra bedroom," O'Neal points out, "they use that as workspace, so there's no privacy [for the guests]."

01 A movable wall, built on a custom pulley-and-track system, creates an instant guest room in the space between the kitchen and the bathroom.

02 Inside the guest room is space for a queen-sized bed. Leather paneling absorbs sound, ensuring a good night's sleep.

02

As such, AvroKO didn't want to build a second bedroom that would inevitably get filled with a desk and computer, or act as a giant walk-in closet. Instead, their solution was to create a flexible room within the 655-square-foot studio that adapts to houseguests when necessary. "We called it the 'guest room cubby.'" In short, a movable wall was built on a custom pulley-and-track system that creates an instant guest room in the space between the kitchen and the bathroom. When out-of-towners are visiting, the wall pulls out to reveal a 70-square-foot room, fit with a queen-sized bed. Without the visiting guests, the wall pushes back and the room is "put away." »65

03

04

Engineering the movable wall was no small feat. "This was the trickiest piece of the space," says O'Neal. In fact, they designed the motorized structure and tore it apart again and again to get it operating smoothly and without any noise. The third time proved to be the charm. The side that faces the kitchen is very functional. It includes essential kitchen appliances like a stainless-steel KitchenAid refrigerator and microwave-oven unit. The wall is ordinarily pushed back as far as it will go to maximize the kitchen space.

On the guest room side, a queen-sized bed is tucked flush to the wall with custom-built latches. "Everything's custom," O'Neal says of the apartment's interior. When the bed is needed, it unfolds horizontally and provides ample sleeping space. They also built two niches in the walls: one for pillows and blankets and one for storage of a reading lamp and reading materials. To finish off the guest room, leather paneling was added to help with sound reduction. "One of the challenges we wanted to address was the difficulty New Yorkers faced when hosting guests and offering them some privacy and also the sound transference between apartments," O'Neal says. "The leather panels were part of that solution."

03 The far wall of the kitchen looks hip with its stainless steel appliances. What you can't see, however, is that the wall is built on a motorized pulley-and-track system, pulling out to reveal an extra bedroom. Smart!

04 The movable wall is ordinarily pushed back to maximize the kitchen space, but you can see the depth offered to the guest room behind the wall when it's pulled forward.

06

05

The flexible features of smart.space don't end with the guest room. The team took advantage of 12-foot ceilings to install a loft workspace, removing an often-messy area from the tranquility of the living area. By doing this, they also maximized square footage in the main room, which, by day, is an open living room for entertaining and relaxing. At night, a custom-built Murphy bed, yet another convertible feature, pulls out to reveal a comfy Tempur-Pedic mattress. To keep the compact studio uncluttered, AvroKO created custom-built cabinets along the entry wall to stow seasonal items, like folding Dahon bicycles. And as a nod to yesteryears, there's even a built-in, foldout ironing board. »68

05 By day, the studio's main room is wide open for entertaining and relaxing. At night, the custom-built Murphy bed with a Tempur-Pedic mattress pulls down for sleeping.

06 The view from the loft workspace reveals a stylish home chock full of space-efficient functions.

07

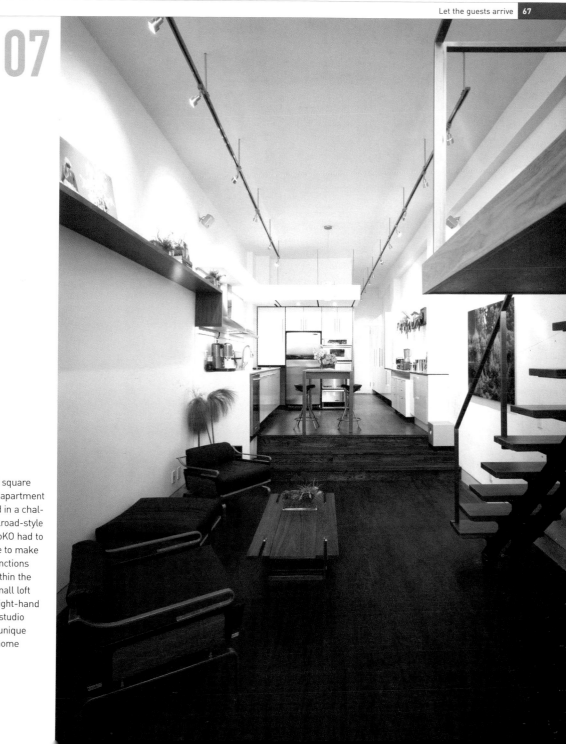

07 The 655 square feet of this apartment is arranged in a challenging railroad-style layout. AvroKO had to get creative to make multiple functions possible within the space. A small loft along the right-hand side of the studio provides a unique area for a home office.

To top off their creative space-saving solutions, AvroKO added style-conscious and environmentally friendly details. The smart.space apartment, which the firm intends to roll out in New York and beyond, boasts features such as simplehuman bag collectors—compact and chic containers for plastic bag recycling—and energy-efficient Koncept lighting. "When designing with an eye towards space efficiency, we thought, 'What other ways can you improve an individual's lifestyle?'" reflects O'Neal. "There's a way to maximize square footage and just be a lot more intelligent about it." In other words, there's always room for "smart.space."

08 To keep the small studio uncluttered, AvroKO created custom-built cabinets for storage of items like folding Dahon bicycles.

08

**SMART.SPACE
SHOWS US:**

» Maximized square footage for multiple functions.
» The transformation from living to sleeping space.
» Built-in storage units and loft to maximize apartment's vertical space.

DESIGN FIRM: AvroKO
FOUNDED: 2000
MEMBERS: 17
ADDRESS: 210 Elizabeth Street, New York, NY 10012
PHONE: 212.343.7024
FAX: 212.343.1072
WEBSITE: www.avroko.com
DRIVING PHILOSOPHY: We are more interested in an all-encompassing idea, look, and feel than one particular design vehicle. We are also deeply interested in how design affects its inhabitants or viewers on a psychological level.
PHOTOGRAPHY: Yuki Kuwana and Michael Weber

Light sculpting

Inside Outside/Macken & Macken
Leefdaal, Belgium
4,413 square feet

When Petra Blaisse surveyed the open first-floor plan in this house being built by architects Macken & Macken, she knew there was an opportunity to do something striking. The dramatic light flooding in the floor-to-ceiling windows, which extend nearly wall-to-wall, seemed to be waiting to be harnessed and recast. "The surrounding landscape of fields is really amazing," says Bart Macken, principal of Macken & Macken. "The client wanted a house with an open relation to the landscape but at the same time, a lot of privacy and the possibility to withdraw."

Enter Petra Blaisse, the creator of Dutch design firm Inside Outside. Known for her pioneering work using soft materials to reconfigure spaces while »74

01

02

03

01, 02, 03, 04, 05 The owner wanted a home that would capture views of the stunning open fields of the surrounding Belgian countryside from every room.

Photos © Paul Casaer

05

04

06

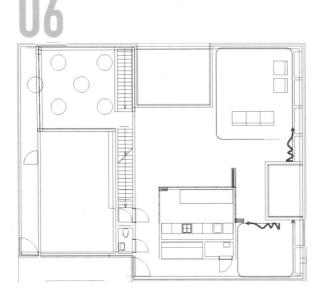

07

06 The floor plan for the first floor: two sets of curtain walls define the two main living spaces.

07 To change the relationship between the interior and exterior spaces, Inside Outside created an opaque curtain that would envelop the room and add warmth.

08, 09 While the wall-to-wall glass windows provide breathtaking views of the countryside, the strong sun can be overwhelming during the day. Curtains help to regulate the temperature and the use of varying fabrics like silk and a metallized fabric from Verosol (a sheer fabric woven with aluminum to reduce glare and deflect heat) create a visual landscape inside.

Photo 09 © Paul Casaer

adding movement and visual excitement, it was in designing theaters that Blaisse learned how to use fabric to transform and add dimension, attracting partnerships with some of the most celebrated names in current design, including Rem Koolhaas.

For this home in Leefdaal, Belgium, Macken & Macken brought Inside Outside onto the project to create a "house-within-a-house."

They had designed the home with a wealth of fluid space to create as open of an orientation to the views outside as possible. They now tasked Blaisse to come up with a program that would control privacy, regulation, intimacy, and acoustics within the interior.

Using the strong light that flooded the home from all sides, Blaisse set about sculpting the space with a series of six curtains that

08

09

would manipulate the interior into fluid rooms. The strong, clean lines of the modernist home created the perfect canvas for layering on the softer shapes and textures that fabric could add.

To define the living room, Blaisse designed a curtain divider from multiple panels of fabric. The curtain is formed from panels of bold fuchsia silk and muted gray velour, interspersed with sheer panels of a Verosol

metallic, a fabric woven with aluminum to reduce glare and deflect heat. The peek-a-boo panels frame views of the Belgian countryside and create windows where light can pour in. During the course of the day, shadows shaped by the gaps in the curtain create an evolving lightscape across the floor, ceilings, and walls. The sheer panels allow light and sight lines to penetrate the room while also creating a clear

separation of space when drawn. The curtain is particularly useful when the owners are watching television. The fabric helps to regulate glare and bounce sound back into the room. Hung on a track in the ceiling, the curtains can quickly be pulled into a bundle in the corner, opening the space back up to the rest of the house.

Across from the living room, the kitchen benefits from a hard form of a curtain

10

11

wall. Macken & Macken designed a series of folding panels constructed from translucent honeycomb lined with lime green Lucite. The panels form three sides of the kitchen so that when completely retracted, the kitchen footprint can become part of the main living space. Using the same flooring material in the kitchen as on the rest of the ground floor helps to tie the spaces together. By organizing all of the kitchen's appliances and workspace against one wall, the kitchen's impact on the floor plan can be minimized to a single corridor »78

10, 11, 12 Hinged Lucite panels form three sides of the kitchen, allowing it to be open to the rest of the first floor or closed off as a separate room.

Photos © Paul Casaer

12

when not in use. When extended, the panels create a translucent green box that forms a full-sized kitchen.

The weight of the fabrics Blaisse chose dramatically alters the effect she created in each room. To separate an office space from the surrounding corridors, Blaisse employed a curtain made from a heavier weave of a Verosol fabric. The treatment still allows the space to feel open and airy, yet gives enough definition to outline a working space that is distinct from the surrounding walkways. The furniture is kept sparse, with the main statement being restricted to shelves that extend from »80

14

13 The large windows in this home allow tremendous light to penetrate the core of the home. Panels woven from Versol fabric help to reduce glare and keep the home a moderate temperature.

14 A sheer curtain designates a specific area for the home office, while maintaining open sight lines to the spectacular view beyond. The built-in shelves that span the back of the house from side to side help to create a visual break, defining the edge of the room.

Photo © Paul Casaer

one end of the house to the other in front of the expansive windows. Small arrangements on the shelves help to create breaks in the views and some sense of a visual stop at the edge of the house.

Upstairs, in the more private spaces of the home, Blaisse was able to be even more experimental. Here, she began layering multiple curtains to create an even greater variety of effects. The first layer she used is a sheer voile that helps to reflect the strong light. A band of more opaque fabric running along the bottom gives weight to the curtain wall and obscures the hard edges where the floor meets the walls. The next layer is a bright magenta velour that helps to regulate light and

acoustics. The last layer is Markilux, a fabric mainly used outdoors to create sails and awnings. In the first bedroom, bright pink suns appear on the velour during the day when sunlight pours into the room through large circular cutouts in the Markilux. In the second bedroom, a row of circular cutouts in the velour allows the dark brown Markilux to show through. Small pinholes cast constellations of light onto the dark hardwood floors.

Throughout, the hard, modern lines of the house balance beautifully with the soft, playful qualities of Blaisse's material interventions. The fabrics Blaisse selected add tactility and warmth, while their curvy shapes and pops of color add a touch of whimsy. It's the final dressing this house needed to feel complete.

15

16

17

15 Depending on how tautly the curtains are drawn, the homeowners can further change the pattern and texture the fabric creates. Stretched out in full, the curtain becomes a rigid plane, and where there is more slack, pleats create a more delicate effect.

16 Pinholes in the Markilux channel sunlight into bursts of light on the floor.

17 The use of three layers of fabric in this bedroom creates a spectacular array of effects. When the sheer voile, magenta velour, and brown Markilux curtains are all drawn, the incoming light becomes dazzling pink spotlights on the dark wood floors.

**LEEFDAAL HOUSE
SHOWS US:**

» A layout effortlessly changed for different activities by using curtains.
» A large expanse broken up with different panels of fabric in varying weights and colors.
» Curtains of varying weights layered to create different effects during the day and night.

DESIGN FIRM: Inside Outside
FOUNDED: 1991
MEMBERS: 10
ADDRESS: Eerste Nassaustraat 5, 1052 BD Amsterdam, The Netherlands
PHONE: 31.20.6810.801
FAX: 31.20.6810.466
WEBSITE: www.insideoutside.nl
DRIVING PHILOSOPHY: We specialize in the rare combination of both interior and exterior design, interweaving architecture and landscape. Our projects not only change their architectural context by introducing visual and sensual effects, such as color, flexibility, view, seasonal change, and movement, but they also function to solve acoustic, climactic, shading, and spatial necessities.

DESIGN FIRM: Macken & Macken Architecten BVBA
FOUNDED: 1993
MEMBERS: 4
ADDRESS: Amerstraat 161, B-3200 Aarschot, Belgium
PHONE: 32.16.572.371
FAX: 32.16.572.325
WEBSITE: www.mma.be
DRIVING PHILOSOPHY: We do not hide behind loud statements or gestures to propel our choices. Ours is a subtle language of design that can be converted into effective projects as a result of a lucid understanding of the design brief and an exceptional mastery of a range of design instruments.

Living on wheels
LLEDO CONDE LOFT

Deborah Berke Interiors
New York, NY
4,000 square feet

Restrained and subtle are two of the words most frequently referenced in relation to Deborah Berke's work. From the architect's own mouth, you're likely to hear something more radical like, "I aspire to understatement," or, "Repetition destroys the preciousness of things." Her firm belief in the power and beauty of the ordinary, as well as design that becomes more interesting with time has etched an important space in the architectural landscape for Berke's work.

While her portfolio now includes a large number of retail and institutional clients, Berke is still interested in the home. For a young bachelor moving into a quintessential New York City loft, replete

01

with exposed brick walls, Berke found an interesting laboratory for her ideas.

Young, single, and versatile is how Berke's client described his life, and the way his home should feel. He wanted to be able to host a party in a wide-open space by night and have a full-sized home office at the ready the next morning. Yet, since this was by no means his last move in the city, he didn't want to invest in a lot of design that was uniquely tied to the space. To create this kind of functionality within the confines of the 4,000-square-foot apartment, Berke had a unique solution: make the entire apartment mobile.

From the bed to the dining table to the couch, the entire apartment lives on castor wheels, allowing for split-second transformations to the layout. The apartment is »86

02

01 The few fixed pieces of furniture in the apartment are mounted to a wall in the main living space. Berke installed four shelving units for additional storage, with sliding screens on two to hide less attractive items.

02 Since this active homeowner's spatial needs change hourly, Berke gave him the ultimate flexibility in his floor plan by making everything in the apartment mobile, including the bedroom.

set up to function for two kinds of settings: the single guy and the single guy with ten of his closest friends.

The centerpiece is a 20-foot-long custom titanium table that's built to withstand everything from hot mugs to occasional use as a bird's-eye perch. Pushed against the windows, it becomes an oversized bar and buffet. More often, the table is wheeled into the center of the room for large dinner parties where the host shows off his culinary skills for friends and family.

When food is not the focal point, the owner gravitates to his custom couch, the perfect size for kicking back and watching soccer. By lowering the movable back, it transforms into a club-style lounge seat that can be accessed from both sides. Add some sheets and it can accommodate two guests.

Since Berke enjoys the repetition of simple elements in a space, she restricted »89

03 The 20-foot-long custom titanium table easily seats fourteen. Its massive scale helps to balance the soaring ceiling height.

04 A birch-ply media cabinet hides the TV behind sliding panels, allowing it to blend in with the rest of the apartment when not in use. Circles are subtly incorporated into the design of the apartment, from the castor wheels, to the classic Fortuny lamp, to the rounded pulls on the cabinetry, to contrast the more severe lines in the space.

05 The movable back on this custom black neoprene and felt couch can be lowered to convert into lounge seating or to function as a guest bed.

03

04

05

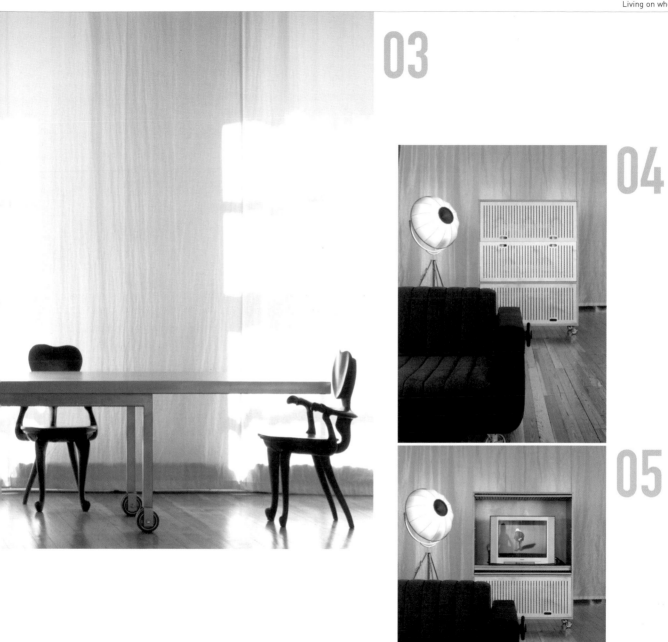

06

06 Above the custom workstation, a metal ledge allows the homeowner to constantly change what's on display as he requires. A shelf below the desk holds essential equipment like the printer, fax machine, and modem, helping to free up more of the work surface.

07 To create a mobile, fully functioning office, Berke built a system of interlocking shelves that pull apart to reveal open and closed storage. The pieces can be configured to form dividing walls to enclose the office area, or they can be pushed against the edge of the room to get them out of the way.

07

the material choices to Baltic birch plywood, titanium, and black metal to tie this apartment together. All of the cabinetry and the shelving in the apartment were custom built from birch ply. To help the home easily transform functions, a cabinet was constructed for the TV with a sliding panel that hides the equipment during off-hours.

The same birch ply houses the extensive home office. The owner, who works from home in graphics, requested a big desk and lots of storage. To keep the workspace from dominating the apartment, Berke created the office-in-a-box. Three interlocking cabinets separate to reveal open and closed shelving. The device allows the office to

expand and fill up half the footprint during working hours and hide away as a discreet wall of cabinetry the rest of the time. The entire apparatus can be rolled anywhere in the apartment thanks to industrial wheels.

In tackling where the owner would sleep, Berke was challenged to find a way to give the owner a private,

intimate area within the open apartment. Not wanting to interrupt the open box with an awkwardly proportioned room, Berke devised a mobile sleeping platform that is essentially a self-contained bedroom.

Under the mattress, three large drawers provide ample space to hold linens and clothes. Depending on his mood or the need to be closer to the air-conditioner, the owner can move the bed to any part of the apartment. It even has built-in privacy screens that lower from the top frame, helping to create a cozy nook in the large-scale apartment.

With so many rigid lines in the apartment and the rigorous editing of materials, Berke wanted to restore softness to the apartment. As such, she installed flowing, white floor-to-ceiling curtains across the wall of windows and added a panel that can be drawn across various portions of the apartment to create divisions of space and form smaller rooms.

The uniformity of color and texture (titanium, Baltic birch plywood, and black metal) creates a modern and masculine feel in the apartment without having to use typically male materials like glass and chrome. It was a way for the owner to get his bachelor pad in a unique space that also manages to have warmth. Each object has a simple function, but the details of the design and the custom applications combine to create an extraordinary effect. And the best part of the design? He can take everything with him when he's ready to move on to the next place.

08

09

08 A self-contained bedroom on wheels, the bed was fitted with three large storage drawers and pull-down privacy shades that create an enclosed space for sleeping.

09 To balance the austerity created by the stern lines of the furniture and the strict color palette, Berke introduced whimsical notes like the Antonio Gaudi–designed dining chairs and installed flowing, white floor-to-ceiling curtains that span the windows and form an interior curtain wall.

LLEDO CONDE LOFT SHOWS US:

» One space can function comfortably for one person or ten. Convertible furniture is key.

» Wheels allow for quick floor plan changes.

» When the solution is in the furniture instead of the home, you can take everything with you when you move.

DESIGN FIRM: Deborah Berke & Partners Architects LLP
FOUNDED: 1982
MEMBERS: 35
ADDRESS: 220 Fifth Avenue, New York, NY 10001
PHONE: 212.229.9211
FAX: 212.989.3347
WEBSITE: www.dberke.com
DRIVING PHILOSOPHY: Drawing on the everyday, the work is understated, intelligent, rich, but unpretentious.

Not just another day at the office

Roger Hirsch Architect, LLC
New York, NY
600 square feet

As the principal of a graphic design studio, it makes sense that Wing Chan has a discerning eye and good taste. So when he bought a 600-square-foot apartment in the West Village of Manhattan that was to be both bachelor pad and company headquarters, he wanted an architect who could deliver an uncompromising solution. He chose well with Roger Hirsch.

"Our challenge was to somehow create for Wing a home and an office, but not have him sacrifice for either one," Hirsch explains in the plainest of terms. "He needed to conduct business—have office meetings and have clients over—and yet he needed to live in this space as well." Flexing his own creativity, the idea Hirsch arrived at with his associate partner,

Myriam Corti, was a very artful and unique one.

For years, Hirsch has collected the kind of old engineering rulers that retract
and fold neatly. He was
inspired by this concept of
something that is extremely
compact and functional but
that can unfold and transform
into something else. He and
his team used this idea as the
basis for creating an office
hidden within a 13-foot-long
by 8-foot-high freestanding
box. After they removed an
existing wall in the apartment, they placed the large
structure in the center of
Wing's apartment. This
returned the division of the
living room and bedroom but,
more than that, offers an
entire home office that can be
hidden from sight.

"Every day, Wing unfolds
the cabinet and opens it up
into a work space," Hirsch
explains of the two large

bi-folding panels that peel
back and provide Wing access
to this secret room. "It's an
automatic office." Inside is
everything a small graphic
design studio could need: two
workstations with oversized
computer monitors, printers,
desk space, plus shelving and
file cabinets for storage. In
fact, Hirsch and his team left
no detail out: they also built in
magnetic strips on which
Wing can hang and track his
current projects.

The box, built of maple-
wood, is solid on all sides
save for one cutout that lets
in light from the apartment's
windows. A low, built-in
bench that acts as both a sofa
and guest bed, is attached to
the outer wall that faces the
living room. When the box's
panels are pulled back, it
glides away and is concealed
from view. Once the workday
is over and the doors are
closed again, the sofa returns
to its original position and
provides a spot to relax in »97

01

01 Two large bi-folding panels fold back and open up the home office, which boasts two workstations and office-supply storage.

02 A cutout in one of the box's walls allows natural light to radiate inside the home office.

02

03

04

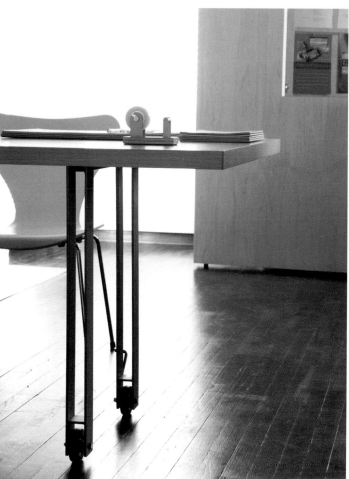

the living room. Not only does this restore a more casual at-home mood, but everything associated with work is put away. "Not one wire cable or computer is visible," says Hirsch of the structure in its closed position. "It's all concealed within the box."

Extending the duality of home and office throughout the apartment, Hirsch set the dining room table on a track and casters. If one of Wing's employees needs the space to work, the table pushes up against the kitchen wall and becomes a third desk. But at night, when Wing is home eating, it rolls to the center of the

03 When Wing needs an extra workstation for one of his employees, the dining room table pushes up against the wall, becoming more work oriented.

04 With the simple placement of casters on the table, Wing can reconfigure his space according to his needs.

05

room and acts as a dining table with chairs on either side.

And because every good office—and home, for that matter—needs plenty of storage, Hirsch spread his craftsmanship throughout the compact apartment. He built custom maplewood cabinetry in the living room, and he extended one existing closet upwards, which gives Wing a place to stash his belongings without eating up valuable floor space. Finally, storage drawers were built beneath the bed for clothing and personal items.

"I really give a lot of credit to Wing to be brave enough to go with this idea," Hirsch says of his unconventional solution of a giant structure in the middle of a small apartment. "He had a lot of faith and trust to say, 'Let's do it,' and that's a rare breed of client." It sounds like a great working relationship, indeed.

06

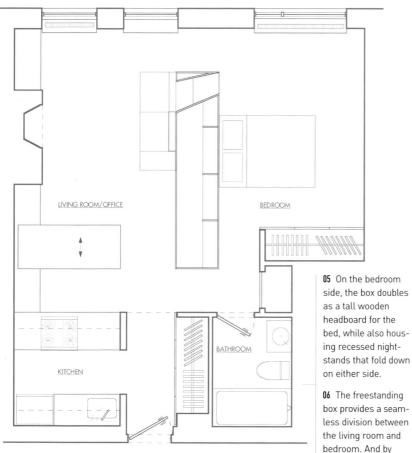

LIVING ROOM/OFFICE

BEDROOM

KITCHEN

BATHROOM

HOME/OFFICE
SHOWS US:

» Literal transformation
from living to working.
» Movable furniture that
accommodates multiple
functions.
» Discreet storage areas.

DESIGN FIRM: Roger Hirsch
Architect, LLC
FOUNDED: 1991
MEMBERS: 4
ADDRESS: 91 Crosby Street,
New York, NY 10012
PHONE: 212.219.2609
FAX: 212.219.2767
WEBSITE:
www.rogerhirsch.com
DRIVING PHILOSOPHY: To take
the site and client's program
as the starting point and turn
constraints into opportunities,
creating designs that are both
functional in use and imagi-
native in concept.
PHOTOGRAPHY: Minh + Wass

05 On the bedroom
side, the box doubles
as a tall wooden
headboard for the
bed, while also hous-
ing recessed night-
stands that fold down
on either side.

06 The freestanding
box provides a seam-
less division between
the living room and
bedroom. And by
peeling back the bi-
folding panels, a
"secret" room is
revealed inside.

Bold moves in São Paulo

Isay Weinfeld
São Paulo, Brazil
3,068 square feet

Architect Isay Weinfeld's designs make as bold of statements as the bronzed bodies decorating São Paulo's famous beaches. Also an award-winning filmmaker, he has a keen eye for forging connections between the indoors and outdoors and creating environments that usher in the gorgeous weather and lush scenery of Brazil. Often cited alongside Oscar Niemeyer, Weinfeld has distinguished a new wave of architecture in Brazil, making him a favorite among local movie starlets building the perfect stage for parties as well as commissions elsewhere in the world.

The young fashion designer who asked Weinfeld to build this home for him had taken it upon himself to scout the neighborhood in search of appropriate examples of his ideal home. Weinfeld recalls, "He

01

thought the best thing to do was to perform 'on-site research' around the city, so he took his bike and rode about, taking pictures of houses he liked." The two became acquainted through a mutual friend and, at their first meeting, Weinfeld agreed to design the young man's house within the first few minutes of sitting down. When the client asked, "How can you make such a commitment knowing nothing about me?" Weinfeld responded that most of the photos the man took were in fact residences he had designed.

While each of Weinfeld's designs is strikingly different, there's an undeniable thread running through them: he always finds a way to beautifully connect the indoors and outdoors. After all, when you

live in a climate like the one São Paulo is blessed with, you want to make the most of every breeze and plot of green. For the lucky many who pass through its doors, Casa Cinza is a study in living simultaneously inside and outside. For the socially inclined owner, a space for lavish entertaining was top of mind. Says Weinfeld, "There was a wish for great integration of the social area of the house to its gardens, so we opted for big sliding doors."

The ones that have guests gasping when they walk in the front door are spectacular 16-foot-high glass panels that open the entire rear of the home to the garden. The ground level feels more like a covered pavilion than anything you would call a traditional living room. Polished cement floors feel cool and casual underfoot and extend the motif of indoor/outdoor »104

01 A 16-foot-tall wall of glass greets you as you enter the main living space. The entire back wall of this home consists of three sliding panels of glass that allow the north facade to become completely open, letting the sights, sounds, and smells of the garden flow freely through the house.

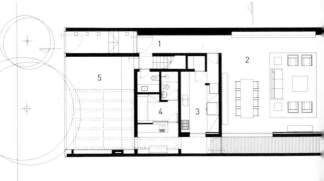

living. A type of finish you might find on a patio, the treatment makes it feel like you're shuffling around outside while you're indoors.

As the main focus in this space is entertaining, the first floor is an open cube that invites circulation and ease of movement. The unobstructed ceilings lend drama and excitement to the space, enhancing the chatter of guests milling about. To take advantage of the ideal Brazilian climate, the owner usually leaves the sliding doors open, extending his living room out onto the swath of green lawn outside. White stucco walls at the edge of the property keep out strong breezes, while also guarding the space from noise and neighbors. Even on rainy days, the large panes of glass allow the room to visually extend to the back of the garden, making the home feel open and airy.

The owner also wanted the option of having a more intimate connection to the outdoors off the dining area. Weinfeld incorporated smaller glass panels that are the height of a regular room on the east side of the house. When you're seated and looking out toward the small side deck, it is as if you're dining by a small courtyard at a restaurant. A lone vine trailing the exterior wall creates a lovely outdoor painting.

The petite side yard is the perfect size for guests to spill out onto while sipping cocktails or taking in a coffee or cigarette after dinner. It also makes it easy to dine alfresco every night. By throwing open the sliding panels, the dining room feels like it's outside. With the two sliding walls working in concert, breezes can circulate throughout the home and the space stays comfortable, even on hot days.

When the guests have all headed home and the »106

02

03

02 With two walls that open to the exterior on the ground floor, on a warm summer day the living space feels more like an enormous covered porch than a formal living room.

03 To contrast with the loud statement of the glass wall in the back, a more intimately scaled side deck extends off the dining area. The timber-clad portion of the mezzanine juts out past the sliding doors by the dining area. The line helps extend the illusion of the merging of indoor and outdoor space.

04

05

owner wants a cozier space to retire to, he heads upstairs to the mezzanine-level den. Clad in reclaimed wood, it allows the second story to be open to the rest of the house, while also creating a more enveloping space with lower ceilings where the owner watches television or reads in the evenings. On the edge overlooking the first floor, a spun-steel fireplace hovers from the ceiling, attached only by its flue. In this way "it wouldn't look like a heavy element on the mezzanine, blocking the view," explains Weinfeld. In another balancing act, a set of cantilevered, cement-faced steps lead from the den up to the bedrooms on the top level.

Weinfeld's cinematic flair allows him to create startlingly lovely *mis-en-scènes* in his homes. In each room of Casa Cinza there is a statement being made, whether it is through a wall of glass, a floating pit of fire, or a scene of quiet beauty like the vine climbing the side yard wall. For Weinfeld though, it is not about expressing his own voice in the design; the statements he makes are inextricably tied to the client. "My thinking in each project is very particular and attached to one client's wishes and demands. What I consider to be fundamental, whatever the change involved, is that the result greatly reflect the client's personality—the architect is just assisting in finding the way to express it."

06

07

CASA CINZA SHOWS US:

» Large sliding doors extend your living space outside.
» Using traditionally exterior materials inside helps to merge the indoors and outdoors seamlessly.
» In an open plan, a mezzanine level creates a cozy space to retreat to.

04 The private spaces in the home have a distinctly different personality from the public rooms. Here, on the third floor, the bedroom is intimate and subdued.

05 The low ceilings of the den enhance the warmth of the room and create a quiet transition point between the public space in the house and the private bedrooms upstairs.

06 Underneath the reclaimed timber–clad mezzanine are the kitchen and laundry areas. Not needing 16-foot ceilings in these spaces allowed Weinfeld to stack the den on top of these rooms.

07 Hovering over the edge of the mezzanine, the Ergofocus, produced in France and made from steel, is suspended from the ceiling. The piece rotates 360 degrees, allowing it to be the focal point of the den or a floating display of fire from the ground floor.

DESIGN FIRM: Isay Weinfeld
FOUNDED: 1973
MEMBERS: 20
ADDRESS: Rua Andre Fernandes 175, São Paulo, 04536-020, Brazil
PHONE: 55.11.3079.7581
WEBSITE: www.isayweinfeld.com
DRIVING PHILOSOPHY: What moves me is the new, the challenge. So I do not want, ever, to become a specialist—in whatever the subject.
PHOTOGRAPHY: Rômulo Fialdini

A trio of uses for a movable cube

MESH Architectures
New York, NY
3,300 square feet

It's a now familiar story: an old warehouse gets converted into housing. How do you design the space for
residential needs and comfort? Do you maintain the
open lofty feel or create conventional rooms? Do you
leave the original character intact or lay over it with
traditional elements? How do you maximize lighting,
privacy, and storage? When Eric Liftin and his wife
moved into their downtown Manhattan loft, they faced

these questions and issues. But as the founder of the
interdisciplinary architectural firm, MESH, Liftin also
had bright ideas and quick solutions at hand.

One of the first actions Liftin took in the converted
warehouse was installing walls to create privacy. One
of these walls runs the entire length of the loft on a
diagonal. "It is set so it maximizes the bedroom in
the back while also opening up towards the front to

01

02

04

take advantage of the river views," explains Liftin of their westward-facing home over-looking the Hudson River. Within the wall, which is Lumasite—a fiberglass-reinforced acrylic—on the front and maple veneer ply-wood on the back, two differ-ent kinds of lights are embedded. Low, ambient bulbs create a soft glow at

night, and fluorescents are a more utilitarian option for daytime. At any hour, the wall offers a clean, uniform look. But closer to the front of the home is one significant interruption.

Liftin created a small library, the Cube, that fits snugly into the diagonal wall. From the center of the loft, it appears as a semitransparent

panel that conceals shelves and objects on the other side. But when it's pulled out, an entire 8 x 8-foot room is revealed. "We move it out periodically to entertain visi-tors or ourselves," says »113

03

05

01, 02 The 8 x 8-foot Cube fits seamlessly in a wall that glows alternately by ambient and fluorescent lighting.

03 When pulled out just a little, the Cube transforms the space by acting as a light fixture and visual display.

04 The diagonal wall that runs through the loft is a main feature of the home's layout, opening up the back bedroom towards the front river views.

05 The translucent Cube easily rolls out on casters, but is too heavy to move inadvertently on its own.

06

07

08

06 The converted warehouse seamlessly features new materials like the wood floors and lightbox wall, and original elements such as the raw support pillars.

07 The interior of the Cube is designed to be intimate and conducive to many activities. "It is by most standards a tiny room, but it has everything necessary: comfort, stimulation of books and video, and peace."

08 Thanks to a curtain wall and the Cube's mobility, the Liftins' home maintains a constant fluidity that opens up to the need at hand.

Liftin. "Its lightness and mobility inspire a sense of possibility and make a room-sized structure feel like furniture."

The Cube's interior is lined with birch plywood shelves and outfitted with a video projector and surround sound. "It was originally a place to go read, draw, or think about things—sort of like a little meditation room," Liftin reflects. Wired for lighting and electricity and outfitted with soft surfaces for comfort, it also offers some serious functionality. "I bought some gym mats for the floor and a wedge of medium-density foam for the back bolsters, and it's all covered by synthetic fur," he says. "The nice thing about it is you realize you don't need a lot of space to do something very satisfying."

The Cube not only offers a quiet place to read or watch movies, it also separates the

his and her studies that reside behind the wall. "It has multiple functions," Liftin explains further. "It's a room, of course, and it's a room divider. And it's also a lighting fixture because when the light is on, it glows like a lightbox and illuminates the room." Since Liftin often finds himself working on projects at home, and his wife, who's a writer and professor, also needs a workstation, this flexible solution works perfectly. It's consistent with the openness of the loft, and also allows their adjoining studies to be separated and reunited simply by shifting the Cube in and out of position.

Setting up for peace and intimacy is a definite theme in the Liftins' home. While they created distinct rooms and areas of use, the loft still

09

10

manages to feel airy. Along the main entrance, for example, a curtain wall obscures the studies, but it can remain open to make the entryway larger and more inviting.

The same holds true for the bedroom, which is separated from the bathroom by only a parachute-nylon curtain. Most of the time, these two spaces are united, opening the bathroom to sunlight

and communication between it and the sleeping quarters. But the curtain is drawn at night for a serene environment. "I don't really want to look at the shower when I'm drifting off," Liftin confesses.

11

THE CUBE SHOWS US:

» Intimate confines within a large-scale home.
» A multifunctional, movable room.
» Separation of space and corresponding uses.

DESIGN FIRM: MESH Architectures
FOUNDED: 1997
MEMBERS: 4
ADDRESS: 180 Varick Street, 11th Floor, New York, NY 10014
PHONE: 212.989.3884
WEBSITE: www.mesh-arc.com
DRIVING PHILOSOPHY: MESH integrates the interaction of people and information into an architectural experience, bringing electronic, networked media into the design process.
PHOTOGRAPHY: Frank Oudeman

09, 10 When the Cube is in position, it separates the his and her studies. When it's pulled out slightly, it is also the perfect projector throw distance to watch movies from inside.

11 Another convertible feature in the home is this duo-tone curtain wall. It can be left open to enhance the loft style, or pulled close to create a focused room for working.

The lives we lead today call for rooms that accommodate multiple functions so we can get maximum usage.

Curtains are one of the easiest and most flexible ways to partition off a room.

Since many homeowners alternately want open space and privacy, a wall that pivots can offer both.

02

Successful strategies for getting more bang out of your blueprint

Movable walls

SHIFTING YOUR FLOOR PLAN

Photo © Paul Warchol

Photo © Michael Moran

Pivot, slide, swivel, and fold—it sounds like a dance. And in a sense, it is. These are the ways that movable walls function, proving to be one of the most impactful devices you can use for extra flexibility. Because you can arrange movable walls to suit your spontaneous or long-term needs, they offer infinite opportunities to be multifunctional. Movable walls create aural and visual separation, as well as aesthetic and functional delineation. They offer constant transformation and fit seamlessly within a home, whether it's a traditional or modern structure. And it is all up to you to adjust each of your walls however you wish.

01

Slide into place. Think about how you want to use your movable wall: Will it separate and define space? Create multiple functions or, conversely, condense them? Will it be used daily or only on particular occasions, like when guests visit? Answering these questions will help choose the wall that's right for your home. Depending on the method of installation, it can provide different benefits. Walls that slide on tracks from the ceiling or floor can open up one side of the room to completely change the floor plan. Or they can slide into a wall, like a pocket door, creating open space. Other options include something that folds against a perpendicular wall like an accordion, or pivots outward on an axis. »122

01, 02 To provide fluid functionality in a renovated Manhattan apartment, CR Studio inserted a sandblasted acrylic partition that, when moved right, extends the kitchen area into the living room. The wall slides left to carve out a niche within the entry foyer and allow the occupants to close off the kitchen. Note the castors on the furniture, which offer another layer of convertibility.

Photos © Peter Margonelli

02

03

Room within a room. Just as movable walls allow you to draw a line between the functions of two rooms, they also give you the power to switch roles within the same room. A sliding wall can section off a changing area within a bedroom, for instance, or a study for the parents can be hidden within a family playroom. The room can be altered to your needs, whether those needs change on an hourly basis, or only once a month. You can make the space work for you, not against you. »124

04

03 This panel system, fixed to the floor and wall with offset pivot hinges, separates a guest bedroom from a double-height gallery space in a large New York City loft. Made of water-white glass in wood frames, the panels easily pivot to help modulate sound and privacy, while maintaining the airy sophistication of the home.

Photo © Paul Warchol

04 To get a sense of spaciousness and flexibility without a fully moving wall, New York–based architect Andrew Franz uses pocket doors. In this town-house, a wide pocket door was the perfect solution for a basement that sees many uses. As Franz says, "It allows for an open family area . . . permitting the room to function as a study, guest room, or future bedroom."

Photo © Michael Moran

05

A little privacy, please. Since many homeowners alternately want open space and privacy, a wall that pivots can offer both. A sliding fabric screen or solid panel that swivels from the ceiling offers variable degrees of seclusion in unique, fluid forms. Beyond the type of wall and how it functions, consider the materials used. While an acrylic panel or fabric screen each offers some measure of transparency, the acrylic partition will be a better choice for soundproofing. A glass wall offers visual continuity but can deflect noise. And finally, wood and metal walls create distinct separations between spaces, visually and aurally. »126

05 Substantial screens offer the ultimate flexibility: walls that leave the residence with you. Brooklyn, New York–based designer Matthew Gagnon implemented his slotted maple screens in a local artist's loft that "needed to be a full-time home, part-time art gallery, and occasional entertainment space." The screens provide openness and natural light, but also enclose an area and designate its use—in this instance, a dining area.

Photo © Matt Gagnon

06

06 Eric Liftin of MESH Architectures created an entire 17 x 12-foot library in the middle of a loft by installing two movable walls of shelves. The left-facing wall slides back on its axis, while the wall on the right swivels on a hinge. When both of these walls are moved, they open up to reveal an inner sanctum. Conversely, when the walls remain fixed, the loft has a closed, intimate feel.

Photos © Frank Oudeman

From open to intimate and back again. When we talk about convertible houses, the whole idea is design that gives you expandable options and increased functionality. With one movable wall, you can choose between a large, community-oriented space, or two or three smaller, more intimate areas. Think about a rectangular parlor, for example. A sliding wall in the middle can be closed, giving you a living room on one side and a separate dining room on the other. But by leaving the wall open, you can increase the space and merge the rooms' functions. Instead of one sliding wall, you can even implement a series of moving partitions, allowing you to define and designate the space several ways.

Platforms and mezzanines

GAINING SPACE OVERHEAD AND UNDERFOOT

While most of us are inclined to think of expansion as building an addition onto the back of the house or moving into a larger home, sometimes you can find more living space just by looking up.

The same thing that made tree houses and the top bunk so appealing growing up, lend loft living its adult charm. Climbing up top still gives you that feeling of getting away from everything on the ground and disappearing into another world.

How low can you go? In a home with tall ceilings, a mezzanine floor can create an entire suite of rooms from untapped vertical space. If your ceilings are at least 12 feet high, you have enough clearance to add

01

a mezzanine level. There are some areas that make better partners for your new overhead addition than others. It's best to position mezzanines over rooms that are conducive to shorter ceilings, such as the kitchen, where it's an advantage to have a smaller space to ventilate and a dropped ceiling brings task lighting closer to the work surface. Bathrooms, home offices, and closets are also good choices.

What's the appeal of mezzanines?
You may be asking, if you have enough space to add a second floor, why not just build a second floor? There are several considerations that make a partial floor addition more attractive. Mezzanines can take advantage of using metal floors

rather than a traditional beam floor, reducing the floor thickness from one foot to half a foot. Rather than eating into the square footage of the ground floor for supports, mezzanine floors are often suspended from the roof. They're also less expensive to build and, depending on where you live, local building codes may not allow you to install a full additional floor in your existing home. Most important of all, you've waited all this time for your chic urban loft, the last thing you want to do is pilfer all your open space in order to add a new floor on top. Mezzanines help preserve a feeling of spaciousness by creating a more transparent addition that also retains double-height ceilings in the rest of the space. »133

02

01 Try to locate mezzanines above spaces that benefit from having lower ceilings. In this Wimbledon home, Terry Pawson Architects built a lounge area over the kitchen, preserving the double-height ceilings over the dining area. The lower kitchen ceiling brings lighting closer to the counter and makes the space feel cozier.

Photo © Jeremy Cockayne /arcaid.co.uk

02 For those who aren't prone to claustrophobia or bed rolling, creating a sleeping platform is a great way to slot in two rooms' worth of function into one space. Maria Speake of Retrouvius and architect Joanna Rippon created this floating bedroom for a young photographer in Camden, London, whose studio is located on the ground floor. With just enough room for a mattress and an alarm clock, the device frees up the space below for models and stylists prepping for the day's shoots.

Photo © Henry Wilson /Redcover.com

03

03 In this home for a photographer and a journalist, a lofted office space is located over a guest room. Visitors can still have privacy, but you don't waste prime living space for an area that only sees part-time use. Careful integration of the sliding panels covering the doorway make the guest room nearly invisible when not in use.

Photo © Ton Kinsbergen /Beateworks/Corbis

04 While the rest of this home by architect Isay Weinfeld is dominated by towering 21-foot ceilings, a mezzanine creates more intimate quarters for the bedroom. Sliding panels can completely close off the room to create a place to hide away.

Photo © Rômulo Fialdini

05 For her own home, architect Sarah Featherstone used mezzanines to create distinct zones within the apartment. By leaving the floors open to each other, the rooms still have a strong sense of connection. She maximizes the space underneath the staircase leading to the lounge area with built-in storage and a wall nook.

Photo © Tim Evan /Redcover.com

04

Getting cozy. While there may not be any dividing walls in the rest of the home, a mezzanine room helps you create one space in an open floor plan that has a sense of intimacy. It's nice to have a den or bedroom with normal ceiling heights when the rest of the house feels large and vast. No matter how much you like entertaining in grand spaces, as humans we like to nest and have someplace to retreat that feels more protected.

Moving on up. Platforms create both visual and physical separation, a useful way to help organize space. The act of stepping up or down is a powerful cue that you're moving into a new area. In the same way that walking up onto a performance stage elevates that space for a special function, by creating different levels of living in your home, you assign distinct zones to each space. You might locate a home office on an upper level to isolate it from the noise and activity on the ground floor, or place a playroom on its own platform to give children a place to go that feels like their own.

Do you need more storage? Maybe you don't need an entire addition overhead; you might just need a few extra square feet to make space for all your stuff. Creating a storage platform for out-of-season things and infrequently used items gets them out of your way. If you don't have room to build something above, you can put it underfoot. Putting your bed on top of a platform makes way for pullout drawers and cabinetry underneath. This kind of storage works well for heavy items or things that are awkward to lift. A taller platform can create space for a wall of cabinets or even additional closets.

05

Put it to work. If you're looking to get more living space, you have to make sure you're capitalizing on every last usable square inch. Stairwells are an excellent example of dead space that's often overlooked. The area under a staircase is the perfect place to build out cabinetry or shelving. A wider-than-usual landing is a great place to put a desk and convert a pass-through area into an airy "room." And what if you have an awkwardly shaped roof or a funny little dormer? Adding platforms and access ways can create a wonderful little retreat in an otherwise untapped space.

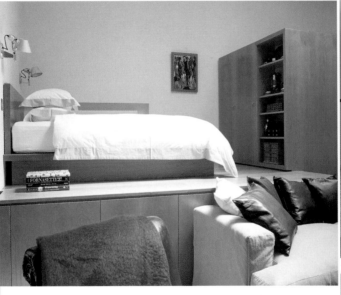

06 When your ceilings aren't tall enough to build a mezzanine overhead, a low platform can give you the extra space you need. In this apartment, designed by architect John Wright for industrial designer Dan Black, a large platform separates the bed from the living area, while creating loads of storage underneath.

Photo © Henry Wilson /Redcover.com

07 Architect Steven Holl carved out pockets of livable space in the peculiar upper reaches of this home in New Mexico.

Photo © Paul Warchol

*tip*archive

» You need ceilings at least 12 feet high to add a mezzanine level.
» Building a mezzanine floor from steel takes up only 6 inches of height versus the 12 inches required for a traditional floor.
» If you have lower ceilings, consider a low-profile platform to increase your storage space.

Curtain walls

FLEXING YOUR ROOM OPTIONS

Photo © Winfried Heinze/Redcover.com

Photo © Silent Gliss

How many of us remember sharing a room with a sibling and draping a sheet between the beds to separate our space from theirs? Curtains are one of the easiest and most flexible ways to partition off a room.

Many of today's open space plans are a dramatic way to show off the house when friends are over, but not necessarily ideal for day-to-day living. Whether you are a household of one or six, you need your

space to perform a variety of functions and it's not always practical for those activities to occur in one big, open area.

Appearing and disappearing rooms. Curtains are a simple way to section off a room and reduce the scale of a space. Visually, curtains can create a boundary to close off one area from the rest of the home. You can create a divider that still allows light, sound, and air to circulate. In a wide-open space, curtains can define a living room or an office in one section of the floor plan when drawn, providing a specific place for an activity to occur. By enclosing the area, curtains give you a way to break up the volumes in a large space. Unlike standing walls, however, curtains can easily be pulled to one side, instantly converting two spaces back into one when you're entertaining or craving open views.

Functional curtains. In an oversized room, curtains can create a sense of intimacy in an otherwise cavernous space. Curtains can function in a number of ways depending on the weight and type of

material used. Tall ceilings and no dividing walls are a recipe for chilly, drafty spaces. Floor-to-ceiling curtains in a medium to heavyweight fabric make individual rooms that are smaller and easier to heat. Similar to the idea behind medieval canopy beds, curtain walls help trap heat in more contained spaces. Adding a layer of thermal paneling makes this even more effective.

A heavier curtain can also serve to block out light and sound. Rather than creating a windowless media room that's only used on movie nights, a curtain made from a dark-colored velvet can create a light-free viewing room and close off a space to optimize a surround-sound system. Lightweight materials »140

01

01 Curtain walls don't have to feel billowy and romantic. A pull-down shade, or in this case slatted blinds, can create a crisp, contemporary room divider.

Photo © Winfried Heinze/Redcover.com

02 In the large master bedroom of this couple's Manhattan loft, architect Richard Gluckman used a soft white curtain to enclose a more intimate space around the bed.

Photo © Fernando Bengoechea/Beateworks/Corbis

02

03

can be lined with blackout fabric specially designed to prevent any light from seeping through. If there is someone in your home who is sensitive to sunlight, this same treatment can be applied to create a secondary wall in a bedroom or in any other part of the house.

Make it sing. Curtains can be much more than just a space divider, however. You can radically alter the mood of a room by drawing a curtain across the space. A transparent wall of fabric can beautifully filter strong light to create a warm glow throughout the room. Or, when you have a minimal backdrop, curtains can be layered against it to add richness. Sheer, gauzy curtains can be used to soften the view, while a second curtain in a heavier fabric can create a play of shadow on top.

To break up a large expanse of space, you can alternate panels of fabric in various materials or create a band of sheer fabric at the top to let light pass through. Curtains in lighter materials can be used for a softer effect, suggesting a division of space rather than drawing a defining line. A more formal installation can be achieved with a material like copper mesh or beaded strands. Completely sheer curtains can signal a change in space without visually closing off any volumes. To heighten the sense of drama in an adjoining space, a curtain »143

03 A sheer black curtain between the bathroom and living room in art collector Cindy Gallop's loft creates a theatrical transition between the two rooms.

Photo © Michael Weber

04 New York design firm The Apartment used a heavy velvet curtain to section off a screening room in this Manhattan loft.

Photo © Michael Weber

04

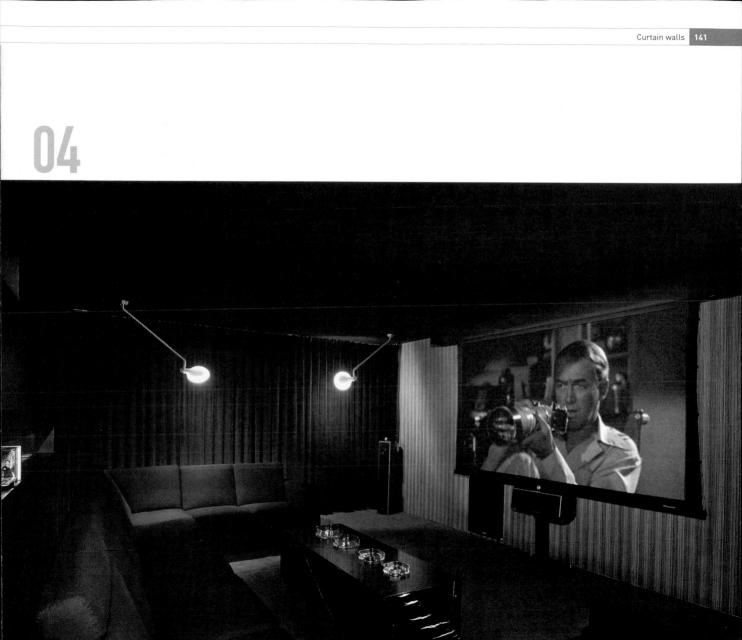

05

05 The first floor of this home by architect Isay Weinfeld in Morumbi, a district of São Paulo, is an open pavilion that connects the expansive living room with the pool outside. Curtains help to define the space and offer some privacy while allowing the scents of the garden to waft in.

Photo © Leonardo Finotti

06 Inside Outside designed this custom ceiling track to trace a sinuous curve that reflects the shape of the design on the fabric itself.

06

made of a transparent material provides a soft veil over the contents within.

Where you thought there wasn't room ... Whereas you're usually limited to right angles and straight lines when constructing a room with two-by-fours and drywall, you can design a curtain wall with curves and bends, following the shape of an unusually proportioned room or creating a silhouette that contrasts against straight walls. Because of their fluid form, curtains lend themselves to flexible formations.

There are other practical advantages to choosing

curtains for a space divider. In a smaller home, the thickness of a dividing wall would eat into valuable floor space. Or the layout of the room may not allow for a door to swing out into the space. And there are many people who simply prefer the smoother, quieter operation of sliding open a curtain versus the more jarring action of opening and shutting a door. However you choose to make use of them, curtain walls are an easy and valuable tool for creating convertible living.

*tip*archive

Thinking of installing a curtain wall? These are a few options that work well.

Ceiling tracks. Ceiling tracks are the most common mechanism for mounting curtain walls and can be laid out in a variety of configurations, allowing you to customize where each bend occurs.

Wire suspension. Done well, a wire strand can create a streamlined, modern look. Make sure you select a hanging device that stands up to the weight of the fabric you choose to avoid sagging.

Curtain rod. The simplest application can be done with a regular curtain rod. Installed on the ceiling rather than on a wall, it also allows you to use standard curtain panels.

Professional installations. There are a number of more high-tech options available. Silent Gliss offers several variations, from curtains that retract into the ceiling to swiveling fabric panels. The benefit of bringing in a professional solution is a wider array of installations and fabric choices that result in a more polished-looking application. www.silentgliss-usa.com

Indoor/outdoor

MERGING INSIDE OUT

>>

There's a reason why staring out the window is such a popular way to daydream. A view to the out-doors is a chance to connect with everything that's happening in the rest of the world. If you're cramped for space between your four walls, your stay-at-home escape may be waiting just outside your back door.

A room with a view. Getting creative with your outdoor space is a smart way to gain flexibility in your home. The best indoor/outdoor spaces not only take advantage of the added physical space available when you merge interior and exterior, but use the open views from the outdoors to expand the visual space indoors. Linking the two spaces via

01

windows and sliding panels can change how the outside is felt from the inside and vice versa.

The key is locating windows and doorways where they'll frame a fantastic view, drawing the eye out past the borders of the house. Depending on how large of an opening you create, you can blur the line between indoors and outdoors completely. Locating a window low to the ground, for example, allows you to feel like you can step right out to the other side. And with today's window casings and glass manufacturing techniques, it's not only possible, but reasonably affordable, to install windows the size of small walls in your home.

Let it flow. Once you've gone to the trouble of creating these fantastic views, don't make the mistake of putting, say, your TV cabinet right between your new windows. To help the eye move beyond the immediate room, it's »148

01 Two walls of sliding panels wheel away to open up an entire corner of the first floor of this home by Isay Weinfeld in Morumbi, Brazil. The result is a dramatic pavilion-style space that creates a seamless transition between the indoors and outdoors.

Photo © Leonardo Finotti

02 Jacques Van Haren infused this house in Brussels with glass to open up the interior to the lush greenery outside. Off the living room, a wall of glass makes the seating area feel as if it were carved into the lawn outside. A pivoting glass panel allows the doorway to blend perfectly with the stationary glass panels when shut.

Photo © Jacques Van Haren

02

helpful to eliminate visual barriers and distractions en route. The trick is to get rid of anything that's competing for your attention with the sights outside.

One helpful rule is to keep furniture low to the ground so there's a clear path to the outside. Any techniques you would apply to link two rooms in an open floor plan inside can likewise help create a seamless flow between the interior and exterior. Repeating shapes and elements from one room to the next also helps tie spaces into one another, as does choosing a similar flooring material. Continuous architectural lines, be it an interior wall that becomes an exterior wall or keeping the floor the same level inside and out, will also create a smooth transition. And there are many choices in stone, wood, and cast materials like cement that work just as well inside your home as they do when exposed to the elements outside.

Making the connection. While everything we've discussed so far can benefit you with the feeling of extra space year-round, if you're lucky enough to have attractive outdoor space and temperate weather, pushing your living space out past the boundaries of your home's footprint is a fantastic way to gain more square footage.

One of the most common ways to connect the indoors and the outdoors is with a sliding glass door. Most of us remember the bulky, metal-framed, vacu-seal versions we grew up with. Now, engineering advancements have created excellent new options that span from floor to ceiling, from one side of the house to the other, essentially opening up an entire wall of the home to the outside. When paired on two sides of the house, it's possible to instantly convert a living room into an open breezeway.

To create a dramatic connection to the outdoors, about two large sliding doors at the corner of the home. When both panels are open, the room takes on the atmosphere of an open-air pavilion and the space is instantly expanded to two, three, or even fours times the volume. The open corner creates a striking focal point that allows the interior to expand in two directions.

A solution that gives you more control over the degree of openness to the exterior is pivoting doors. Rotating on single axes, you can turn multiple panels like the louvers on a shutter, funneling breezes to different parts of the house and helping to control the temperature. When they're rotated to ninety degrees, they disappear from view entirely.

For a wide span of space, hinged doors that fold »151

03

03 Large sliding panels open up the northeast corner of this home in Santa Monica, California, designed by JFAK Architects, to the wraparound koi pond. The generous opening allowed the owners to trade in air-conditioning for cooling breezes.

Photo © Benny Chan/Fotoworks

04

05

back like an accordion are a smart choice. They fold flat to the sides of the house allowing you to open the horizontal space to its fullest. This is also an easily adaptable stock option. Regardless of the size of your opening, much like adding or removing links on a watch, it's possible to customize a prefabricated solution to the size of your home.

But what if your space is narrow enough as it is? Any side-to-side solution will create some bulk at the edges of the doorway. If your room is slim from left to right, look to the garage for your solution. The same mechanisms that raise your garage door can be used to hoist an entire wall in your living room overhead and out of the way.

Depending on your climate, local traffic patterns, and mood, there might be times when you want your indoor space to feel more contained. In the way that shutters protect windows during storms, building a set of

04 In this oceanfront home off the coast of Brazil, Isay Weinfeld employs a wall of pivoting doors to create your choice of entrances to the deck and pool outside. The doors can be rotated to any position, allowing the entire room to be open to the outside, or just a portion. Horizontal slats in the panels echo the horizontal lines of the shore and skyline beyond.

Photo © Tuca Reinés

05 In this home in Antwerp, Belgium, META architectuurbureau installed two sets of folding doors to open the main living space to the outside deck. The folding doors mimic the lines of the windows on the second floor, maintaining a streamlined profile. The track for the sliding doors is sunk into the ground so there is a seamless transition between the indoors and outdoors.

Photo © Toon Grobet

06

solid panels that can slide over your doors and windows can block out overpowering light or keep frosty chills at bay in the wintertime.

Let there be light. Another idea that has long been used to bring light and air indoors is the interior courtyard. Located in the center of the house and open to the skies above and the house on all four sides, a courtyard allows light to penetrate into the center of the house. Large plates of glass allow the airiness of a planted courtyard to permeate the rest of the house, while sliding panels allow the courtyard to temporarily join with the living room, dining room, or office. If your home faces busy streets on all sides, this is one way to create a private outdoor space that you can merge with your indoor space.

07

06 In this master bedroom, obstructions to the right, left, and front (stairway on the left, windows on the right, narrow walkway in front of the bed) meant the doorway to the outdoor space had only one direction to go— up into the ceiling.

Photo © Richard Powers/Redcover.com

07 Marpillero Pollak Architects created a flexible solution for joining this living room with the backyard. In the extreme climates of Boulder, Colorado, the couple who live here wanted to have full access to the outdoor space during the summer months, and a way to control the light and temperature during the winter months. The solution was two sets of panels. Glass pocket doors slide away to expose an entire side of the room, while a set of wooden panels slide over the glass panels to create privacy and block out excess light at other times.

Multiuse rooms

MULTITASKING AT HOME

Gone are the days of using your living room strictly for reading the newspaper and having a formal salon reserved for special guests. The lives we lead today call for rooms that accommodate multiple functions so we can get maximum usage. Kitchens now spill into living rooms, and guest rooms transform into studies, which transform yet again into playrooms. We've been multitasking for years. It was really only a matter of time before our homes did, too. *Multitasking* is a buzzword we're all personally and professionally familiar with—why shouldn't we ask our homes to be just as hardworking?

01

Single-room dwelling. Studio living is the ultimate study in multiuse space. In one simple room, you're sleeping, working, and entertaining. But there are different ways to create pockets of functionality. To make the sleep area discreet, for example, use a Murphy bed, sleeper sofa, or tuck a futon behind a folding screen. It's all about camouflage. Likewise, you can use one long table for both dining and working, swapping out tabletop materials to accommodate the task at hand. Clever storage devices, like colorful boxes or wire baskets, can contain materials when not in use. Lastly, a simple trick like putting a couch or infinity bookshelves in the middle of the room automatically divides the space, giving you a natural break to the floor plan. »158

02

01 In this Manhattan apartment renovated by CR Studio, the den serves as a family room, guest room, and child's playroom, all in one. A Murphy bed, cabinet that hides the TV, and a closet for guests' belongings all contribute to its multifunctionality, which is enhanced by a trio of pocket doors that offers the option of privacy.

Photo © Peter Margonelli

02 Often more than one member of the household needs to use the computer or office. Even in this small apartment, designer Johannes Knoops was able to fit in two separate workstations. Just big enough to pull up a chair and hop online, the desk is completely concealed when the panel is folded up.

Photo © inside & out

03

Doubling up. While most homes have more space than a studio, the same philosophy applies: let one room do double duty for you. This can be as simple as using a second bedroom as an office (an old-fashioned secretary desk provides natural cover for a messy desktop). Or if you have an especially large living room, place a table and chairs off in the corner, and you've identified this as the dining area. Installing a chandelier overhead or laying a carpet below the table further defines the area. »160

03, 04 At a New York loft that Roger Hirsch renovated with interior designers Tocar Inc., a centrally located, ebony-colored wall offers a sophisticated separation of the open space. But it's much more than that: it also hides an entire guest room. When needed, a full-sized bed folds down and translucent curtains extend, creating an intimate sleeping cove.

Photos © Michael Moran

04

05

Built-in functionality.

Convertible furniture, as we'll see in the next chapter, offers a streamlined way to reorient a room. But custom design takes it to another level. Built-in cabinetry can provide foldout workstations or conceal entertainment systems so the room is functional when you need it, but can be put away when you don't. Also think about building beds or desks in otherwise overlooked areas like walk-in closets or wall nooks that can't accommodate regular pieces of furniture. »162

05 Designer Alessandro Villa arranged the main rooms of this apartment in Monza, Italy, around one central multifunctional area. By placing the family's TV and sound system on swiveling bases, they can be used equally between the living and dining rooms. This provides flexibility for the family and also acts as a fluid room divider—a nice update for the way we live today.

Photos © Gianni Sala

06

Spatial organization. When it comes down to it, you should use your space the way you choose to define it. It might just be the least likely room in the house that is begging to be more functional. Ever think of making the master bathroom a sewing room as well? Or setting up an office in the cozy confines of your kitchen? Don't discount rooms like the bathroom or kitchen—they are utilitarian, after all. And don't overlook the small touches. Think about inlaying a different floor material in a small section of a large room to designate its use. Or simply put furniture on tracking, casters, or swiveling platforms so they shift and perform according to your needs.

07

06 In the same home that got a hideaway guest bed, Roger Hirsch installed another brilliant convertible feature. Along one wall of the living area, a floating teak counter transforms into two individual workstations, thanks to ingenious flip-top desks. Not only does this multifunctional design eliminate the need to devote an entire room to a home office, but when the desks are not in use, the line of the counter helps frame a large projection TV for viewing from the adjoining living room.

Photos © Michael Moran

07 To create a home office and quiet reflection room, plus a place to store a world-class collection of Japanese scrolls, designer Johannes Knoops collaborated with Mr. Hanafuse of Miya Shoji to design custom "origami" cabinets that fold and bend according to the owner's needs. Here, a gorgeous solid maple panel pivots down to reveal a fully functioning desk.

Photos © inside & out

Convertible furniture

When Dan Hisel coined his Z-Box "furnitecture," he really tapped into something. Traditionally, furniture and architecture have served different needs. But as our lifestyles demand more of us, it's easy to see how synergies can be gained by combining the two.

Multidisciplinary designers and furniture makers alike are pushing boundaries, allowing us to consider the pieces themselves and the rooms in which they live in a whole new fashion.

One salient feature about furniture is that it's not attached to a given home's architecture. It can be transported from one residence to another, offering flexible arrangements in multiple homes. With this in mind, pick quality pieces and give thought to the functions you need most, be it storage, display, privacy, or practicality.

01

Space savers. Convertible furniture does wonders for cramped quarters. After all, you're packing two or more functions into one piece and can put it away when you're done. A Murphy bed, for instance, folds away during the day, opening up the room for other uses. A TV or workstation tucked inside an armoire or cabinet can instantly disappear behind closed doors. And a table or couch on wheels can glide into another room, or even be stored inside a closet, giving you back valuable floor space.

01 Jeffrey Warren of Vestal Design created a piece that's at once playful and highly functional: the DoubleSpace Kitchenette. Noticing that people rarely sit while cooking, he overlapped these activities by designing a roomy chair that converts into a convenient countertop with two electric burners. A carefully placed axle allows the perfect sitting height to swing up and become the perfect cooking height. To ensure safety, the burners cannot be turned on while in the chair orientation.

Photos © Jeffrey Warren

02

A twist on the classic. Just as rooms can do double duty, with thoughtful planning, so too can furniture. And not to knock the good old Murphy beds—as the super-chic smart.space apartment attests, they can be quite stylish—but there's a lot more creativity getting folded into the options these days. Tables transform into benches and seats. Beds get built-in entertainment systems. Multidisciplinary designers and furniture makers alike are pushing boundaries, allowing us to consider the pieces themselves and the rooms in which they live in a whole new fashion.

02 Shin Azumi's masterful armchair changes into a table with a simple, smooth action. The solid maple and powder-coated steel pipe materials make it stable for both functions.

Photos © Julian Hawkins

Climb inside. You used to not be allowed to put your feet on the furniture. Now you can walk all over it. Some of the most inventive convertible options act like an extra room. This is an especially smart solution for loft dwellers who have high ceilings and no walls. But the principle works in any type of home—that is, creating a structure that offers privacy for sleeping or a dedicated area for working, without disrupting the room's existing dynamics. »171

03

03 The Celeste bed by Crème Fresh takes the canopied bed to a new level. The canopy stretches over the bed, creating a cozy environment that feels like a room unto its own. And layering in added functionality, a projector can be placed behind the back wall so you can watch movies and play games in bed without needing an unsightly television in the bedroom.

Photos © Kris Van den Berghe

04

Upgrade to a suite. You might want to consider creating convertibility throughout your entire home. Make it a requirement for all of your furniture pieces so you can move seamlessly between rooms and functions. If you're sleeping on a sofa bed, for example, also choose tables, benches, and entertainment systems that fold away. Use an over-sized ottoman as both seating and a table. Or, instead of putting casters on just one table, put your entire home on wheels so you can reconfigure your space for any whim or need.

04 The Dutch design firm i29 created a new interpretation of "bed and bath." At the front of this unit, a sink and mirror were installed, and glass doors give entry to the shower and toilet. Enclosing the queen-sized bed is a sheer voile canopy printed with blossoming tree branches.

Photos © i29 office for design

Small stools create drop-in seating, a side table for drinks, or even a quick stand-in for the stepladder.

When your dinner party swells from four to ten people, move the office desk over to the dining table for an instant expansion opportunity.

Sectional sofas are a great way to configure your space: break them into separate pieces, or keep all sections together in an L-shape so they function as a room divider.

Simple solutions for any type of home

roombyroom
Convertible living

Now that you've seen the pros at it,
    what can you do to add flexibility in your home? A glance through any
design magazine will give you inspiration. Here, we've collected architects' and designers' favorite tricks, great
Web sites, and catalog picks for the cleverest convertible furniture.

Go configure!

Before you begin, here are some things to keep in mind...

Challenge yourself

Don't be afraid to experiment. The great thing about convertible living is that it's designed to be changeable.

"Don't limit yourself to your past. Think long term and towards how you'd like to live, not how you lived before."

—**Andrew Franz, Architect**

"Create a matrix. When your space is limited, it is important to have a strong organizing principle in the space from which all the solutions flow."

—**Alliot Cheng, Designer**

"Go home, look at all your objects and furniture, and ask when was the last time you touched them. A beautiful piece that you love will always have its place in your home. All the rest is superfluous and noisy for the mind."

—**Jacques Van Haren, Architect**

kitchen

A place to work. The kitchen? It's actually the perfect place to put a desk.
You rarely cook at the same time that you pay bills. And this means you'll be making use of
your kitchen outside of mealtimes.

Double duty

We're not in an English manor with a full kitchen
staff to keep five sets of china in rotation. When
choosing dinnerware and serving pieces, select
items that can be used in more than one way. A
sturdy ceramic pitcher can also display kitchen
utensils or a bouquet of tulips. Buy mixing bowls
that are attractive enough to use as serving bowls at
the dinner table (think glass or stoneware).

Elbow room

A simple board that's wider than the sink creates a
second work surface.

Fold down

Look to furniture—be it a table, bench, or seat—that
attaches to the wall and lowers for use and folds
away when you're done to maximize floor space.

Under wraps

"Disguise the kitchen by using under-counter refrigerator and freezer units below custom cabinetry
made of 'non-kitchen-like' material."

—**Johannes Knoops, Designer**

"Maximize space and conceal unsightly clutter in the
kitchen with a pull-out wall pantry with multiple
compartments for items like spices, canned goods,
and pastas. While cooking, the pantry can be gently
pushed away and tucked neatly into the wall."

—**Jennie Nunn, Associate Editor,
California Home and Design Magazine**

dining space

Room for one more. When your dinner party swells from four to ten, it's useful to have a table that can grow with you. Choose a table with extension leaves, or have an extra folding tabletop made to fit over an existing table. For Thanksgiving-size gatherings, a foldout picnic or conference table can be pulled out from storage.
Add a white tablecloth and it will blend in seamlessly.

"Keep space planning open and simple, allowing for objects to be moved at will. For example, if you're having a large dinner party, move the office desk over to the dining table for an instant expansion opportunity."
—**Stefan Boublil, Designer**

"For those who use the dining table as a home office, buy one or two pedestal files on wheels—preferably with two 'box' drawers and one file drawer—and use them to hide away your office when not in use. After working at your dining table, put your laptop computer, files, and supplies in the pedestal file and simply roll into a nearby closet or corner of the room, and it's all hidden from view."
—**Roger Hirsch, Architect**

It's a squeeze
Take a cue from tiny restaurants: a banquette along a wall lets you pack in more seating in a tight space.

The beautiful **X-Pand System** table is essentially an accordion-style tabletop that extends the surface to make space for extra dinner guests. And you don't have to find storage space for expansion leaves. www.xpand-furniture.com

bedroom

Go far out. If you build a platform bed, extend the platform. You can make it reach a little farther to act as a shelf for books and knickknacks, or an exaggerated extension provides room for seating or a table.

Underfoot
Storage platforms under the bed make space for bedding, linens, and all those extra sweaters.

Breakfast out of bed
What to do with that awkward leftover space in oversized bedrooms? Create a reading area with two armchairs and a taller side table, which can double as an intimate spot to have breakfast with your partner.

Flou's Salina bed, designed by Rodolfo Dordoni, is chic and sneaky. In addition to the practical shelf cubbies that allow you to display books and knick-knacks, the mattress opens up like a clam to reveal extra storage beneath the bed. www.flou.com

His and hers
An attractive table in the bedroom can transform daily from vanity to desktop. Store makeup and cufflinks in a few drawers and the checkbook and laptop in another.

The portable vanity from the **Conran Shop** with its dozens of tiny drawers and compartments plus a three-way mirror makes this a fully functional vanity. But when closed, it all gets conveniently tucked away and the cabinet looks like a sleek retro piece of luggage. www.conran.com

living room

Hideaways aren't just for Murphy beds. Think: sofa beds, armoires that conceal desks or entertainment systems, or built-in desks that fold out from cabinetry. Anything that hides its function when not in use.

Slice the couch
Sectional sofas are making a comeback and they're a great way to configure your space. Break off pieces into separate chairs, or keep all sections together in an L-shape, which also functions as a room divider.

Where to put the guests
A sleeper sofa is more "adult" than a futon and less of a financial commitment than a Murphy bed.

Borrow a time-tested solution from the Japanese, who have perfected the art of compact living. Futons are rolled away and stored in closets during the day, creating valuable living space. While this may not be a solution for everyone, it's a functional alternative to a guest bedroom and much more comfortable than an air mattress.

"Window seats can be easily converted to extra sleeping quarters by putting a trundle underneath."
—**Alison Spear, AIA**

"Invest in a stylish Murphy bed. They can be hard to find, but they make space ultimately flexible!"
—**Kristina O'Neal, Designer**

The Bingo Pouf from **Design Within Reach** is an ottoman when folded up, a coffee table with the addition of a tray that slides over the top, and when guests arrive, folds out into a sleeping mat. www.dwr.com

How convertible can you go? La Literal, a bed from the Spanish firm **Sellex,** can be bunk beds, a folding bed, a double bed, and a studio. It's smart contemporary design features metal vertical supports and epoxy painted colors. www.sellex.es

On-the-go seating
Stack floor cushions against the wall in a nice assortment of Lifesaver colors. They brighten up the room and provide extra seats.

Small stools create drop-in seating, a side table to hold your mug, or a quick stand-in for the stepladder. Try the Yanagi Elephant stool or **Philippe Starck**'s La Boheme stool for Kartell.

The **Vessel Squat Bench** is a multipurpose piece that can be used as a bench, a table, or stacked and used as shelving. Each module includes two natural aluminum legs that offer a convenient place to store books and more. www.vessel.com

DWR's Nexus Storage Cubes, designed by GRID2 International, offer 19 x 18 x 18-inch storage capsules that look smart and sophisticated. A cushioned leather top allows the capsules to function as a stool or ottoman. Or flip the top to reveal a wooden tray for use as a side table.

The bamboo lattice stool from **The Container Store** does double duty as a secret storage unit. Similar models are available such as the EVA storage stool, with faux-suede finish, and the Pandan Storage box, which offers a cushy seat. www.containerstore.com

Three-in-one

When space is tight, a bar-height table works great as a desk with an extra long work surface that doesn't protrude too far into the living room. It also, as the name implies, does double duty as a bar. And when you have guests over for potlucks, voilà, it becomes a buffet.

Give 'em a rest

Upholstered ottomans are chicly convertible: they offer rest for weary feet, extra seating for company, and with the addition of a tray, a place to rest your drink.

Design Public's Blythe Ottoman is large enough, firm enough, and flat enough to act as a coffee table. But it's so pretty, you might not want to cover it up. www.designpublic.com

Sofa beds

Pietro Arosio's Sliding Sofa from **DWR** combines uber engineering and comfort. By day, the 28-inch-deep sofa is a sleek, modern place to sit and relax. At night, the backrest folds down into a two-person, queen-sized bed.

The Twilight Sleep Sofa by Flemming Busk, another **DWR** find, functions as a single-person daybed but unfolds to fit two sleepers. An adjustable bolster pillow adds more practicality and comfort by allowing you to customize the seat depth. www.dwr.com

The Multy Sofa Bed, a **Ligne Roset** classic designed by Claude Brisson, converts from sofa to bed to sofa again with a simple fold-down feature. www.ligne-roset-usa.com

American Leather's sleeper sofas are a wise choice, not only because they come in standard mattress sizes (most sleeper sofas are a touch smaller than regular mattresses), from twin to king, but they also don't have that annoying bar that inevitably hurts your back and keeps you awake at night. www.americanleather.com

The Flip Flop Sofa from **CB2** (Crate & Barrel's more economical little sister) can be configured into a double bed. But it can also be adapted into a divan, giving you space for sitting and socializing with either the left or right cushion laid flat. The practicality doesn't end there: the Teflon-treated cotton cover can be removed for cleaning. www.cb2.com

The Lounge Sofa Bed by **apt** easily converts to a bed. But while sitting or lounging by day, you can adjust the backrest (short seat/low backrest or deep seat/higher backrest) for extra comfort.

office

I need a place to work. Thanks to wireless routers and tiny laptops, it's easy to set up shop anywhere in the home. These are some devices that make it easier: a side table on wheels makes a quick rolling desk, a breakfast tray creates a table over your lap in bed or on the couch, and a mounted shelf makes a slim desk that takes up zero room when not in use.

Spreadsheets by day, Aunt Mildred by night

Add a sofa bed or daybed to an office. It works just as well for midday naps as it does for out-of-town guests.

"Be adaptable yourself. If the work area is on wheels, move it around. Try the table up against the wall, not in the middle of the room."

—Andrew Franz, Architect

Out of the closet

Convert a closet—be it a mini linen closet or a deep walk-in—to an office. Stack colorful boxes for storage.

Ikea's wall-mounted, drop-leaf Enkoping table, designed by Anna Larsson, offers a nearly 2-foot-square area that was designed for casual meals, but works just as well for typing. When you're done, it folds flat against the wall to save space. The table is made of solid birch, with four snazzy posters to choose from that are revealed when the table is open. www.ikea.com

for any room…

" **Give yourself lots of storage.** Any large volumetric container can serve
as storage, and amassing several identical units will introduce a serial, minimalist aesthetic."

—Dan Hisel, Architect

Hide and seek Give an alcove a reason for being: convert awkward inlets and nooks into storage solutions. Install wall-mounted shoe racks or bookshelves. To keep them out of sight, hide them behind custom drapes.

Multi-play Choose storage options that work in any room. Pharmacy-style metal cabinets work beautifully for kitchen, bath, or living room storage. When you rearrange one room, you can easily move the piece into another. Open cube shelving is another good choice. It works as well against a wall as it does in the center of the room as a divider. Changing the contents on display constantly evolves a decorative element in the room as well.

"Consider vertical surfaces (walls) for combination storage and purposeful built-ins for things such as a bed, electronic appliances, work desk, bar, etc."

—**William Thomas, Interior Designer**

Take one panel of bentwood and use it in any one of six configurations. **The Other Edge's** REV | ONE line allows you to configure multiple bamboo panels into a cube table, low coffee table, laptop or TV dinner stand, magazine rack, bookcase, or several styles of seating. www.theotheredge.com

Room markers and dividers
Subtle entrance Using curtains instead of doors to create privacy still gives you the option to make the space feel more open.

Splash Paint an accent wall to designate an area of a room for a particular use, be it for dining or working.

Middle ground Infinity bookshelves make a great room divider. Place them in the middle of the floor, instead of against a wall. Display your favorite things and section off part of the room.

"Draperies or flat fabric panels on tracks can provide easy room dividers and also soften the space."
—**William Thomas, Interior Designer**

"Place a light behind the translucent curtain and it
transforms into a glowing light source for the room."
—**Roger Hirsch, Architect**

"A wall need not be full height; often a half
partition will accomplish the necessary task."
—**Andrew Franz, Architect**

Flor's modular 20 x 20-inch carpet tiles let you designate spaces for different uses. For example, create
a living area by assembling a grid of carpet squares.
Make a solid block of color or create a loud pattern.

Inhabit's hanging panels offer a fun way to add flexibility to your space. While they allow natural light

through, they also offer a screen for privacy or just
to mark a specific area. The 24 x 76-inch panels
come in cool patterns like retro grids, grass silhouettes, and whimsical flowers. www.cribcandy.com

Portable, flexible, sound-absorbent felted-wool
screens from **Designers Eye** let you create your
own walls and completely reshape your room. The
50-inch-long screens (which come in 57-inch and
69-inch heights) can be connected magnetically.

The 24 x 72-inch **Material Furniture Flipper Screen**
lets you section off a room and devise privacy. The
cutout circles flip out and secure as shelves, giving
you a stable place to store or display things. You'll
find endless combinations for new displays.

The Pivot Screen by **Mebel Furniture** is made of individual frames of acrylic in soothing colors. Pieces are removable so you can configure the frames to be opaque or translucent, blue, orange, or white. www.mebelfurniture.com

A soft, expandable screen, **Paper Softwall** twists and turns—and folds away when not in use. A unique honeycomb structure absorbs sounds and transmits light. Softwall is also modular: felt and Velcro fasteners link walls so you can lengthen as necessary. www.molodesign.com

Use these Web sites for more ideas and inspiration

Apartmenttherapy.com
Archinect.com
Coolhunting.com
Designaddict.com
Inhabitat.com
Mocoloco.com
Trendsideas.com

Directory of architects and designers

Alessandro Villa
Via Volta 26
20052 Monza
Italy
p/f: 039.322.492
www.alessandrovilla.it

Andrew Franz Architect
39½ Washington Square
South
New York, NY 10012
p: 212.505.1992
f: 212.505.1987
www.andrewfranz.com

The Apartment
101 Crosby Street
New York, NY 10012
p: 212.219.3661
f: 212.219.3683
www.theapt.com

AvroKO
210 Elizabeth Street
New York, NY 10012
p: 212.343.7024
f: 212.343.1072
www.avroko.com

CR Studio Architects, PC
6 West 18th Street
New York, NY 10011
p: 212.989.8187
f: 212.924.4282
www.crstudio.com

Crème Fresh
Korte Bist 6
B-2180 Ekeren
Belgium
p: 32.0.478.97.01.83
www.cremefresh.be

Dan Hisel Design
238 Columbia Street, #2N
Cambridge, MA 02139
p: 617.547.3151
www.danhiseldesign.com

**Deborah Berke & Partners
Architects LLP**
220 Fifth Avenue
New York, NY 10001
p: 212.229.9211
f: 212.989.3347
www.dberke.com

Draughtzman
G/F, 39 North York
Siu Lek Yuen
Shatin, N.T. Hong Kong
China
p: 852.2866.2122

Featherstone Associates
25 Links Yard
Spelman Street
London E1 5LX
England
p: 44.020.7539.3686
f: 44.020.7539.3687
www.featherstone-associates.co.uk

Gluckman Mayner Architects
250 Hudson Street
New York, NY 10013
p: 212.929.0100
f: 212.929.0833
www.gluckmanmayner.net

i29
Industrieweg 29
1115 AD Duivendrecht
The Netherlands
p: 31.20.6956.120
f: 31.20.4165.705
www.i29.nl

Inside Outside
Eerste Nassaustraat 5
1052 BD Amsterdam
The Netherlands
p: 31.20.6810.801
f: 31.20.6810.466
www.insideoutside.nl

Isay Weinfeld Arquiteto
Rua André Fernandes, 175
04536.020 São Paulo
Brazil
p: 55.11.3079.7581
www.isayweinfeld.com

Jacques Van Haren
09 Avenue du Vert Chasseur
Brussels 1180
Belgium
p: 32.2.511.54.43
f: 32.2.511.53.88
www.jacquesvanharen.com

Johannes Knoops
415 Grand Street, E-902
New York, NY 10002
p: 212.842.0049
www.knoops.us

John Friedman Alice Kimm Architects, Inc.
701 East Third Street,
Suite 300
Los Angeles, CA 90013
p: 213.253.4740
f: 213.253.4760
www.jfak.net

John Wright
p: 44.014.2442.4101

LeSieur & Thomas
60 South Main Street
Essex, CT 06426
p: 860.767.3545
f. 860.767.2916

Macken & Macken Architecten BVBA
Amerstraat 161
B-3200 Aarschot
Belgium
p: 32.01.657.2371
f: 32.01.657.2325
www.mma.be

Marpillero Pollak Architects
132 Duane Street, #1
New York, NY 10013
p: 212.619.5560
f: 212.619.5561

Matthew Gagnon Studio
1013 Grand Street, Suite 20
Brooklyn, NY 11211
p: 718.384.7724
f: 718.384.6473
www.mattstudio.com

MESH Architectures
180 Varick Street, 11th Floor
New York, NY 10014
p: 212.989.3884
f: 212.989.2335
www.mesh-arc.com

META architectuur bureau
3 Grote Kraaiwijk
B-2000 Antwerp
Belgium
p: 32.03.213.51.60
f: 32.03.213.51.61
www.meta-architectuur.be

Molo Design, LTD
1470 Venables Street
Vancouver, BC V5L 2G7
Canada
p: 604.696.2501
f: 604.685.0342
www.molodesign.com

nendo
4-1-20-2A Mejiro
Toshima-ku
Tokyo 171-0031
Japan
p: 81.03.3954.5554
f: 81.03.3954.5581
www.nendo.jp

Pierre D'Avoine Architects
6A Order Hall Street
London WC1N 3JW
England
p: 44.020.7242.2124
f: 44.020.7242.2149
www.davoine.net

Retrouvius
Trade Warehouse
2A Ravensworth Road
Kensal Green
London NW10 5NR
England
p: 44.020.8960.6060
www.retrouvius.com

Roger Hirsch
91 Crosby Street
New York, NY 10012
p: 212.219.2609
f: 212.219.2767
www.rogerhirsch.com

Steven Holl Architects
450 West 31st Street,
11th Floor
New York, NY 10001
p: 212.629.7262
www.stevenholl.com

Terry Pawson Architects
206 Merton High Street
London SW19 1AX
England
p: 44.020.8543.2577
f: 44.020.8543.8677
www.terrypawson.com

Vestal Design
www.vestaldesign.com